# Gerontology
# &
# Geriatrics
# Collections

The *Special Collections* series, Lee Ash, Editor:

- *Theatre & Performing Arts Collections*, edited by Louis A. Rachow
- *Biochemistry Collections*, edited by Bernard S. Schlessinger
- *Gerontology & Geriatrics Collections*, edited by Prisca von Dorotka Bagnell
- *Science/Fiction Collections: Fantasy, Supernatural & Weird Tales*, edited by Hal Hall

# Gerontology & Geriatrics Collections

Prisca von Dorotka Bagnell
Guest Editor

Special Collections
Volume 1, Numbers 3/4

The Haworth Press
New York

The Haworth Press, Inc., 28 East 22 Street, New York, NY 10010

**Library of Congress Cataloging in Publication Data**
Main entry under title:

Gerontology & geriatrics collections.

(Special collections ; v. 1, no. 3/4)
"Books of interest to special collections of all kinds, compiled by Lee Ash": p.
Includes bibliographical references.
Contents: Introduction, an historical perspective / Prisca von Dorotka Bagnell—The use of gerontological resources, a five year analysis of information dissemination / Willie M. Edwards—Integrating information technology in gerontology, the Andrus Gerontological Information Center / Margaret L. Kronauer, Stewart R. Greathouse, Jean E. Mueller—[etc.]

1. Gerontology—Information services—United States. 2. Gerontology—Information services—Canada. 3. Geriatrics — Library resources—United States. 4. Geriatrics—Library resources—Canada. I. Bagnell, Prisca von Dorotka. II. Title: Gerontology and geriatrics collections. III. Series.
HQ1064.U5G39  1982       305.2'6'0971       82-11697
ISBN 0-917724-53-4

# Gerontology & Geriatrics Collections

Special Collections
Volume 1, Numbers 3/4

## CONTENTS

# Gerontology
# &
# Geriatrics
# Collections

# FOREWORD

We are all getting older, and while we may not improve ourselves as the philosophers hope we might, we have learned, to some extent, what our problems are as individuals in our society and how society can help us to manage them.

Dr Prisca von Dorotka Bagnell, our Guest Editor for this issue, has written an Introduction that provides a survey of the historical background and societal interest so necessary to bring modern consideration of Geriatrics and Gerontology into perspective. She has accomplished her purpose admirably and, in addition, she has gathered an outstanding group of specialist contributors whose papers provide a never-before-seen overall view of some of the more important aspects of the bibliography and library resources of Gerontology and Geriatrics.

We had not planned that this would have to be a double-issue in the first volume of *Special Collections* but present interest in the subject and the excellence of Dr Bagnell's proposals persuaded the publishers that the larger content would be desirable. It is inevitable, of course, that the papers would contain some slight duplication of content. This does not trouble us because we believe that the volume is unlikely to be read from cover to cover but, rather, will be cited article by article, and the duplicated material is relevant to the content of each piece.

Now, with the issues of Theatre, Biochemistry, Gerontology and Geriatrics behind us, we anticipate those of Science/Fiction, Ballet and The Dance, Aeronautics and Space Flight, Banking and Finance. We, the publishers and I, are grateful for the interest and support we have had from specialists and special collections librarians, and we look forward to our opportunities to be of service to the world of scholarship and libraries.

*Lee Ash*
*General Editor*

*Bethany, CT*

*1*

*A Note from the Series Editor*

Due to manufacturing limitations, four papers originally scheduled for publication in *Gerontology & Geriatrics Collections* will be appearing instead in forthcoming issues of the journal *Behavioral & Social Sciences Librarian*:

"The National Clearinghouse on Aging: Information and the National Overview," by Donald Smith, Director, National Clearinghouse on Aging, Washington, D.C.

"Selected Books for a Geriatric Collection," by Frances Flynn, Center for Community Health and Medical Care, Harvard University Medical School, Boston, Massachusetts.

"Selected Resources in Social Gerontology: Book Review and Bibliography," by Dorothea R. Zito, Gerontology Information Program, All-University Gerontology Center, Syracuse University, Syracuse, New York.

"Gerontological Libraries: Objectives, Services, and Collections," by H. Jean Owens, Director, Learning Resources Center, Institute of Gerontology, Wayne State University, Detroit, Michigan.

# INTRODUCTION: AN HISTORICAL PERSPECTIVE

Interest in the phenomenon of aging has been evident throughout recorded history and its historiography can be traced from ancient times. Ever since then, the process of aging has been considered and reconsidered while attitudes toward aging and the aged have been expressed in both favorable and unappreciative terms, age being praised and lamented by scholars and poets alike.

In ancient Greece, Plato in *The Republic*, has Socrates in conversation with Cephalus comment that: "I regard them (the aged) as travellers who have gone a journey which I too may have to go, and of whom I ought to inquire whether the way is smooth and easy or rugged and difficult".[1] Aristotle, interpreting life by the scholastic tenet of his time, in his treatise on *Life and Death*, considers heat to be the breath of life and postulates that "There are two ways in which fire ceases to exist: it may go out either by exhaustion or by extinction... (the former is due to old age, the latter to violence)",[2] and states that "the source of life is lost to its possessor when the heat with which it is bound up is no longer";[3] while Hippocrates prognosticates unpoetically that; "Old persons endure fasting most easily".[4]

Galen, a physician in Rome in the first century A.D., coined the term Gerocracy in describing medical care for the elderly,[5] and offered medical advice to the aged in his work *De Sanitatem Tuendam*,[6] while the Roman Senator Marcus Tulius Cicero in *De Senectute* defined the social position of the aged in ancient Rome and pointed to early ageism with these lines: "But, the critics say, Old men are morose, troubled, fretful, and hard to please; and if we inquire we shall find that some are misers too. However, these are fault of character, not age".[7] The Roman philosopher, Seneca, in his *Letters to Lucilius* in an early delineation of the life cycle noted that:

> Our span of life is divided into parts; it consists of large circles enclosing smaller. One circle embraces and bounds the rest; it reaches from birth to the last day of existence.... Let us cherish and love old age; for it is full of pleasure if one knows how to use it.[8]

Among the contributions to the historiography on aging in Medieval times is a monograph penned in the 13th century at the Medical School of Salerno especially for the King of England. The purpose of the *Flos Medicinae* was to "preserve Man in good health"[9] because it was believed then, as now, that the attainment of a vigorous long life was well worth achieving. Another geriatric work of the times with a modern sounding theme was *The Cure of Old Age and the Preservation of Youth* by Roger Bacon which also focused on the care and prevention of illness in old age.[10] The Venetian writer Cornaro in the 16th century, drawing from personal experience as an octogenarian, expressed a private view on old age in the First Discourse on *A Treatise of Temperance and Sobriety*, when he reflects: "I have ardent desire that every man should strive to attain my age, in order that he might enjoy what I have found, and what others too will find, to be the most beautiful period in life".[11] A few years later, Francis Bacon in *Of Youth and Age* illustrates another point of view: "Men of age object too much, consult too long, adventure too little, repent too soon, and seldom drive business home to the full period, but content themselves with a mediocrity of success".[12]

From Shakespeare's description of seven stages in life in *As You Like It*; "His act being seven ages",[13] to Erikson's eight stages identifying the life cycle,[14] a change occurred in the field of knowledge—a shift from the humanities to the sciences partly because of the further development of the scientific method, and partly because of advancement in social thought. A change also occurred in the role of the aged in society and in societal attitude toward the aged. Until this change the aged had served society as the reservoir of all accumulated knowledge, as collective memory banks, and the exemplifiers of the rule of conduct whereby "they remained living proof that adhering to prescribed modes of behavior enhanced the possibility of long life".[15] A subtle shift occurred first through modern innovations in medical and social practices in the 18th and 19th centuries.

> Physicians, biologists and sanitary engineers, therefore assumed a greater and highly technical role in the studying and advancing of the principles conducive to increasing longevity and improving hygiene. Americans after the Civil War still acknowledged the importance of moral and sensible deportment, but they steadily preferred to rely on the advice of experts rather than the insight of experience.[16]

To these societal transformations need to be added another phenomenon in the 20th century, the bureaucratization of the society itself.[17] Industrialization, the modernization of society, seemed to have an inverse effect on the role of the aged in society because "although depressed prestige of older people is associated with industrializing societies, mature industrial systems appear to support higher prestige for the elderly, especially as cohorts having better education, health and finances reach old age".[18] Such changes in scientific methodology and in society itself are reflected in the focus of the literature on aging by a change in perspective from the humanistic; the artistic (often pseudo-scholastic), to the empirical scientific; and the systematic observation of natural phenomena.

Aging today, as always, is a human condition, but the field of aging is a complex discipline which can be divided into geriatrics, a neologism coined by I. L. Nascher of New York in 1909, the branch of medicine which concerns itself with the clinical aspects of aging; and gerontology, a term used by I. I. Metchnikoff at the Pasteur Institute in Paris in 1903.[19]

The growing interest in the field of aging in the United States and Canada is partly rooted in demographic trends. Sociologically, the United States belongs to the "Old Countries" of the world today.

> The gerontic population of the U.S., those of 65 and over, numbered 3.1 million in 1900. By 1940, the group had tripled in size to 9.0 million. It more than doubled again to 21.1 million by 1970. In the year 2000, the number of persons 65 and over is expected to be about 31 million. Early in the next century (2010 to 2020), the number of persons 65 and over will leap forward (by 9.6 million or 20 percent).[20]

The increase in the number of the aged in this century, and their growing visibility, spurred the interest of the scientific community to study the aged as members of the society. The phenomenon of an increasing elderly population caused researchers internationally to focus their attention on the problems of the aged in the areas of clinical, behavioral, and social concerns. This interest resulted early in the century in the publication of some landmark works, primarily on the clinical aspects of aging; such as C. M. Child's *Senescence and Rejuvenescence* (1915),[21] *Scenescence the Second Half of Life* by G. Stanley Hall (1922),[22] and the noted work edited by E. V. Cowdry, *Problems of Ageing*, published in 1939.[23]

Another response to the growing number of the elderly was the founding of organizations and programs in the public and private sectors to serve the needs of the elderly. The Elizabethan Laws, whereby the responsibility for the old and infirm was accepted by the government, form the basis for the social welfare regulations in the United States.[24] By the middle of the 19th century, private and voluntary organizations also organized programs for the needy, including the aged. In cities such as Philadelphia, New York and

Boston, community agencies and members of the settlement movement offered services to the aged outside institutions.[25] In the 20th century, medicine, having made important progress in the control of infectious diseases, turned its attention to degenerative diseases, resulting in a series of conferences sponsored by the Josiah Macy Foundation, the National Research Council, and the National Institute on Health—the Age of Aging had arrived.

The public sector also began to organize in the 1930s when the Association for Social Security organized a public assistance program for the needy elderly. In the field of literature, two important monographs by Abraham Epstein, *Facing Old Age* (1922)[26] and *The Challenge of the Aged* (1928), called to attention the plight of the elderly in the United States, the only industrial nation without a comprehensive welfare program for its elderly population.[27] This attention brought about the passage of the *Social Security Act* in 1935. The first National Conference on Aging held in 1950, sponsored by the Federal Security Agency, recognized the emerging interest in the societal aspects of aging by forming sections addressing social and economic concerns. In 1958, Congress passed the *White House Conference on Aging Act*, with Conferences held in 1961, 1971 and 1981, focusing on social concerns of the aged. Another federal agency, the *Administration on Aging*, was established by the *Older Americans Act of 1965*. The AOA today is the principle agency mandated to fund some ninety federally supported programs for the aged in the United States. The recently founded *National Institute on Aging* (1974), was established for the conduct and support of biomedical, social and behavioral research and training programs in aging.

Concurrently and working in concert with these federal agencies, the private sector developed in the 1940s scholarly societies and associations supported by interest groups. Leading scholarly societies in the field of aging in the United States and Canada are: the *Geriatric Society* (New York) founded in 1942 whose members consist of physicians and professionals in the health care services interested in the clinical problems of the aged. The *Gerontological Society of America* (Washington, D.C.), was founded in 1945. By 1948, its membership numbered 48. Today the Society totals 6500 and is organized into the sections: the Behavioral Social Sciences; Biological Sciences; Clinical Medicine; and Social Research Planning. Another important private association is the *National Council on Aging* (Washington, D.C.) founded in 1950 and organized into Committees on Energy, Health, Housing, Industrial Gerontology, Media, Public Policy, Religious Institutions, Senior Centers, and Social Security and Pensions. These committees outline the areas of concern in the field of aging. The organization supported by the largest private interest group is *The American Association of Retired Per-*

*sons* (1958) affiliated with *The National Retired Teachers Association* (1947) with a combined membership of over seven million members. In Canada, the *Canadian Geriatric Research Society* (1975) in Toronto plays an important role in supporting scientific research in the field of aging.

Within the training components in the field of gerontology and geriatrics one needs to list the educational programs offered at gerontology centers and universities. "Over the last five years, gerontology has been one of the fastest growing fields of study on American campuses...One survey indicates that 1,275 schools now offer at least one course in gerontology".[28]

The historical development of the field of aging in the United States and Canada spans only some thirty years. The study of aging is therefore a young science which embraces not only the research sector in which individual scientists in geriatrics and gerontology contribute to the field, but also the training component where professionals in organizations and programs offer specialized services to the aged.

After World War II, aging became recognized as an independent field of study with the result that the research output in the postwar years increased prodigiously. According to Birren, at the turn of the century there were but a few books published on gerontology but "the literature generated between 1950–1960 equalled the production of the literature published in the preceeding 115 years...if this continues, it is expected that between 1970–1980 the publication rates will double again".[29]

This volume on special collections in gerontology and geriatrics attempts to illustrate to the reader the diversity of the information resources in the field of aging and the interdisciplinary nature of this discipline. It also brings attention to the complexity of the systematization of such diverse material for the information seeker. The monograph is roughly divided into categories covering private collections, such as the delightful essay by Dr Joseph T. Freeman, a physician and amateur historian on the "why" and "how" of collecting books on aging.

Major subject collections in academic and public libraries, their holdings and services, are covered in an academic setting by Willie M. Edwards, Director of the Library at the Institute of Gerontology at the University of Michigan and for the University of Southern California, by Margaret L. Kronauer, Information Specialist; Stewart R. Greathouse, Information Scientist; and Jean E. Mueller, Chief Librarian of the Andrus Gerontological Information Center. The public perspective is described by Paula M. Lovas, Head of the National Gerontology Resources Center of the NRTA-AARP.

Information systems in aging, such as archives and clearinghouses are treated by Marta L. Dosa, Professor in the School of Information Studies at Syracuse University, in her interesting paper on models for information transfer in both the field of gerontology and health, "The GRIP and HISP Projects." Scientific Archives are reviewed by Susan B. Haberkorn and Michael W. Traugott describing an approach at securing and translating data for the social science user through the National Archive of Computerized Data on Aging (NACDA) project at the University of Michigan.

As aging is a panhuman, global phenomenon, we have added an international perspective with the excellent paper by George Thomas Beall, Associate Director of the Housing Technical Assistance Program of the International Center for Social Gerontology based in Washington, D.C. Beall delineates efforts in developing international formal information systems in Western Europe; i.e., Great Britain, France, Western Germany, and the United Nations.

Ms. Janet R. Bailin from the School of Information Studies at Syracuse University and Ms. Sherry Morgan with the National Cancer Institute in Bethesda, Maryland, present a manuscript outlining bibliographic tools in gerontology and geriatrics. H. Jean Owens, Director of the Learning Resource Center of the Institute of Gerontology at Wayne State University, adds a selected listing of gerontological libraries and their objectives, holdings and services.

This volume is dedicated to information resources in aging in the United States and Canada and lists three Canadian libraries representing academic and public collections in gerontology and geriatrics. Informative papers on the state of the arts in aging resources in Canada are contributed by Ms. Elaine Duwors, Librarian of the J. W. Crane Memorial Library of the Canadian Geriatric Research Society in Toronto; by Mrs. Joanne Gard Marshall, Clinical Librarian of the Health Sciences Library at McMasters University in Hamilton, Ontario; and by Ms. Gale Moore, Library and Information Consultant to the Programme in Gerontology at the University of Toronto. These papers outline the historical antecedents, the scope and the services of these library collections of the field of aging in Canada.

Having brought to attention the scope and diversity of information resources in the field of aging, one would like to return to its human dimension and impress that the aged are we—a little further down the road of life. A favorite definition of old age is expressed by Cicero who considered old age the last scene in the play of life[30] and states; "No, it is a wonderful state. We have, so to speak, served our term of passion, ambition, contention, desire—the whole lot—and now are our own masters and, as the saying goes, we can now live to our hearts desire''.[31] It is the same sage who suggested that civilizations are measured by the honor in which they hold their elders.

*Prisca von Dorotka Bagnell, Ph.D.*
*Guest Editor*

*All-University Gerontology Center*
*Syracuse University*
*Spring 1981*

## BIBLIOGRAPHY

1. Plato. *The Republic*, Book I. (328). Transl. by Benjamin Jowett. Great Books of the Western World. Chicago, Encyclopedia Britannica, 1952, p. 296.

2. Aristotle. *On Youth and Old Age*, On Life and Death and Breathing (20). Transl. by W. D. Ross. Great Books of the Western World. Chicago, Encyclopedia Britannica, 1952, p. 716.

3. Ibid, *On Life and Death* 1, p. 725.

4. Hippocrates. *Aphorisms*. Section I. 13. Transl. by Francis Adams. Great Books of the Western World. Chicago, Encyclopedia Britannica, 1952, p. 131.

5. Freeman, Joseph T. *Aging*: Its History and Literature. New York, Human Sciences Press, 1979, p. 16.

6. Zeman, Frederic D. *Life's Later Years*: Studies in the Medical History of Old Age. In Roots of Modern Gerontology and Geriatrics edited by Gerald J. Gruman. New York, Arno Press, 1979, p. 302.

7. Cicero, Marcus Tullius. *Cato Maior de Senectute*, XVIII. Transl. by W. A. Falconer. Cambridge, Harvard University Press, 1964, p. 77.

8. Seneca. Lucius Annaeus. *Ad Lucilium Epistulae Morales*. XII On Old Age. Transl. by Richard M. Grummere. Cambridge, Harvard University Press, 1934, pp. 67–69.

9. *Regimen sanitatis Salernitanum* (Flos Medicinae) by Henricus Ronsovius. Transl. by Sir John Harington, London, T. Deave, 1624. On Reader Microprint editions of Early American Inprints published by the American Antiquarian Society. Film 999, no. 21609.

10. Bacon, Roger. *The Cure of Old Age and Preservation of Youth*. In Zeman, p. 788.

11. Cornaro, Luigi. *A treatise of Temperance and Sobriety*, added to the Hygiosticon: or, The right course of preserving life and health unto extream old age by Leonardus Lessius. 2nd. ed. Transl. by George Herbert. Cambridge, University of Cambridge. Film 999, no. 15521.

12. Bacon, Francis. *Of Youth and Age*. In the Works of Francis Bacon, II, Literary and Religious Works. Boston, Houghton, Mifflin & Co. n.d., p. 224.

13. Shakespeare, William. *As You Like It*. Act II, Scene VII, The Temple Shakespeare, 4th ed. (New York), McMillan, 1897, p. 50.

14. Erikson, Erik H. *Childhood and Society*. 1st ed. New York, Norton, 1950.

15. Achenbaum, W. Andrew. *Old Age in the New Land*: The American Experience since 1790. Baltimore, John Hopkins Press, 1978, p. 40.

16. Ibid, p. 41.

17. For works on programs and services in the field of aging in the United States see Carroll E. Estes. *The Aging Enterprise*: A Critical Examination of Social Policies and Ser-

vices for the Aged. San Francisco, Jossey-Bass Publ., 1979, and Donald E. Gelfand and Jody K. Olson. The Aging Network: Programs and Services. New York, Springer, 1980.

18. Fry, Christine L. *Aging in Culture and Society* New York, Praeger, 1980, p. 4, citing Donald C. Cowgill. Aging and Modernization, New York, Appleton-Century Crofts, 1972.

19. Freeman, p. 16.

20. *Sourcebook on Aging*. 2nd ed. Chicago, Marquis Academic Media, 1979, pp. 206–209. Citing data from the U.S. Bureau of Census *Current Population Reports*, "Projections of the Population of the United States: 1975 to 2050", Series P-25, No. 601, Oct. 1975.

21. Child, C. M. *Senescence and Rejuvenescence of Life*. New York, Appleton-Century-Crofts, 1922.

22. Hall, G. Stanley. *Senescence, the Second Half of Life*. New York, Appleton-Century-Crofts, 1922.

23. Cowdry, E. Vincent. *Problems of Ageing*. Baltimore, Walham & Wilkins, 1939.

24. Randall, Ollie A. "Some Historical Developments of Social Aspects of Aging" *The Gerontologist*, v. 5, No. 1, Pt. II, 1965, p. 41.

25. Ibid, pp. 41–43.

26. Epstein, Abraham. *Facing Old Age*: A Study of Old Age Dependency in the United States and Old Age Pensions. New York, A. A. Knopf, 1922.

27. ————. *The Challenge of the Aged*. New York, Vanguard Press, 1928.

28. *New York Times*. Sunday, June 19, 1977; Section: Medicine.

29. Woodruff, Diana S. and James E. Birren. *Aging*: Scientific Perspectives and Social Issues. New York, Van Nostrand Co., 1975, p. 24.

30. Cicero, Marcus Tullius. *On Old Age and Friendship*, IV, 49. Transl. by Frank O. Copley. Ann Arbor, The University of Michigan Press, 1967, p. 26.

31. Ibid, XVIII, 63, p. 32.

# THE USE OF GERONTOLOGICAL RESOURCES: A FIVE YEAR ANALYSIS OF INFORMATION DISSEMINATION

Willie M. Edwards

The Institute of Gerontology Library in Ann Arbor, Michigan conducted this study in order to determine the nature of library users. Of particular interest in this study were the location and the selected characteristics of the library's clientele. The term clientele here is defined as anyone who requested information in person, by mail or by telephone, and who was directly assisted by a member of the library's professional staff.

One of the primary responsibilities of the Institute of Gerontology over the last three decades has been the dissemination of information. The Gerontology Library is basic to this dissemination function: In accordance with the mandate from the State of Michigan, the facility is equipped to provide the appropriate resources to support training programs in the subject area and to support academic and field research and service programs offered by the University.

*The Collection*: The library is located in the central campus of the University of Michigan in Ann Arbor within a few blocks of all other major University libraries, and it maintains close ties with the University of Michigan Library System, which is a separate unit. The Institute of Gerontology Library houses a collection of over 8,000 cataloged and classified volumes, 133 journals, 350 newsletters, 2,000 unpublished research papers and extensive vertical files housing ephemeral material. Primarily in Social Gerontology, the library focuses on the areas of economics, social security, pre-retirement and retirement, housing and environment and long term care. Forty percent of the current collection is reference and the remaining sixty percent is circulating. Complementing these resources the library has an international collection which is strong in United Kingdom material; to a more limited extent, it encompasses European and Asian countries. In addition, it has an historical collection of monographs and books dating back to 1725,

Willie M. Edwards is affiliated with the Institute of Gerontology, 520 E. Liberty Street, Ann Arbor, MI 48109.

as well as an archival collection of letters, manuscripts, photographs, films and tapes from gerontologists in the areas of social policy, retirement, social security and developmental psychology. A Pre-Retirement Reference Desk is available for clients researching retirement issues as well as pre-retirement program planners or persons concerned with their own retirement. In addition, the library is a Service Center for Aging Information (SCAN) Microfiche Repository. As such, it holds a collection of 3,100 reports on microfiche from the Administration on Aging's Service Center on Aging.

*Operation*: The library is barrier free and is open to the University community as well as to the public at large from 8:00 to 5:00 daily, Monday through Friday, and the hours of 7:00 to 9:00 three evenings a week. The library is staffed by two professional librarians, one clerical assistant, three student assistants and one retired librarian volunteer.

An open stack system is used so as to optimize access to collections and to encourage individual browsing. All reference questions are answered by members of the professional staff.

All cataloging and classifying tasks are performed by the Graduate Library Technical Services Department, which in turn is a member of the OCLC, Inc. and Research Libraries Information Network (RLIN). All holdings are represented in the University of Michigan Graduate Library catalog so as to provide access to the University community.

## The Study

In this study, besides assessing the size and type of the library's clientele, an attempt was made to evaluate the extent of communication and assistance being extended to the elderly themselves and to persons working on behalf of the elderly. To accomplish this, the study addressed the following research questions:

1. What is the geographical location of the clientele?
2. What percentage of the clientele is located in Ann Arbor, in metropolitan Detroit and other cities in Michigan?
3. What is the percentage of users residing outside the State of Michigan?
4. Where is the largest clientele concentration located with respect to the 10 regions defined by the Administration on Aging?
5. What are the characteristics of the clientele with respect to organizational affiliation?
6. Is there a correlation between the location of clientele and the concentration of elderly populations in the State of Michigan?

7. What are the subjects of the most frequently answered questions?
8. To what extent is there evidence of subject interlocking for questions answered?

*Background of the Study*: Beginning in 1974, the library staff established a systematic record-keeping system for purposes of clientele identification. At the end of each year a progress report was prepared for the director of the Institute of Gerontology including analysis of the subjects of questions and the institutional affiliations of clients. The progress report served to indicate the areas of strength and weakness in the collection, so that if there was insufficient information on a special subject, materials could then be acquired to bring that area up to an acceptable standard.

## Plan for the Study

*Instruments*: Two instruments were used to collect data: (1) The reference question card recorded the name, address and telephone number of the client plus a notation of the reference question. Additional information might be recorded, for example, the audience for whom the information was needed, and the time limit designated by clients for receipt of materials. The status of each client request was noted at the end of each fiscal year. (2) The client analysis sheet classified clients by organization affiliation, location and subject of information in three categories: (a) university or non-university or other type of organization or business, (b) geographical location of client, (c) subjects of the information requests. The extent of subject interlocking was determined through a random sample of ten percent of the total number of questions answered in each year.

## Definition of Terms Used

For the purpose of this study a Reference Question is defined as a prescribed transaction involving direct communication of a professional staff member with a client for the purpose of supplying factual information. Clients are served in person, by mail or by telephone. Reference questions included the following:

1. *Search Question*, involving time and the use of several reference tools often including secondary sources.
2. *Descriptive Question*, involving the client reading or scanning a number of authoritative sources which describe a condition, activity or program.

3. *Statistical Question*, involving the location of a set of data using primary sources. In such cases a photo copy is sent for verification to the client who is communicating by telephone or mail.
4. *List of References*, four or more references on the same subject are located.
5. *Citation Cleaning*, whereby a list of 10 to 50 references are presented by the user with a fair amount of errors to be verified or corrected.
6. *Interlocking Questions*, where a question spans several disciplines and could therefore be answered entirely by the Institute of Gerontology Library or in conjunction with another special library (e.g., the medical library).

Certain types of questions were omitted from the data: Reference transactions—which we define as a series of functions or activities performed by a staff member, usually scheduled in advance for a person or group, such as bibliography preparation, orientations to library resources, or seminars, etc. Non-prescribed and other transactions not included in the study are:

—*Ready Reference*: questions which can be answered with the use of a handbook or some other appropriate source and require little time and no searching.
—*Orientation Sessions to Library Resources*: this includes persons, groups or classes requesting a special session where a member of the staff explains and demonstrates the use of reference tools and other resources in order to assist clients in developing an ability to use the resources.
—*Reader Advisory Service*: where source books are recommended to clients who request background information on aging or some specific subject.
—*Questions that are rejected* or fail to be answered because they fall outside of the subject resource range and capability of the collection. Such are also not recorded.

## Data Collection

The collection of data spanned a period of five years, June 30th, 1974–July 1st, 1979, and presents a total number of 840 questions. Questions were answered as received. No effort was made to solicit, advertise or control the influx of questions. The questions were answered under normal working conditions.

Clients were identified by name, address and institutional affiliation. If, for example, the affiliation were the University of Michigan, the secondary breakdown might be faculty, student, researcher or Institute of Gerontology staff. If the category was another university institution, the name and location were recorded. Clients from non-university institutions were categorized as follows: health related institutions, nursing homes, hospitals, state and local government agencies, national organizations, businesses, libraries and churches.

## Results

*Reference Questions Answered.* As Figure 1 and Table 1 show, between 1974 and 1975, the total number of questions answered was 118. By June 1979 the total number had risen to 840. The data show that from 1976–1977 there was a 31 percent increase (129–169). The next year, 1977–1978 saw

FIGURE 1

NUMBER OF REFERENCE QUESTIONS

ANSWERED BY YEAR 1974–1979

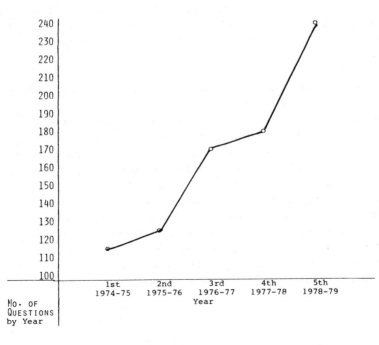

TABLE 1

Number and Increase of Questions Answered by Year

| Year | Number of Questions Answered | Numerical Increase Over Previous Year | Percentage of Increase Over Previous Year |
|------|------|------|------|
| 1974-75 | 118 | | |
| 1975-76 | 129 | 11 | 9.3 |
| 1976-77 | 169 | 40 | 31.0 |
| 1977-78 | 184 | 15 | 8.9 |
| 1978-79 | 240 | 56 | 30.43 |
| Total | 840 | | |

a modest increase of 8.9 percent. From 1978–1979 there was an increase of 30.43 percent, the largest for any year.

*Analysis of Clientele Location.* Table 2 shows that 62 percent of the Institute of Gerontology Library Reference Question clientele in the state reside in Ann Arbor or greater Ann Arbor—within a radius of 20 miles from the campus. The largest number of clients are students and the smallest are the foreign clients. Student use is twice that of faculty. However, usage by the Institute of Gerontology staff is considerable, falling just 4 percent short of student use.

Aside from the University, the largest number of clients in the state reside in the Detroit metropolitan area. Out-of-state clients extending far beyond the University milieu, ranked third.

*Distribution of Clientele.* Figure 2 pictures regional distribution as the regions are defined by AOA. In order not to skew the analysis, this figure does not include the State of Michigan: It shows the distribution of all other clientele, nationally. The largest number of questions answered for a region was 44 for Region 5—Ill., Ind., Ohio, Minn., Wisc. Including the questions answered for Michigan brings this total to 724. The next largest is Region 3—Delaware, Washington D.C., Pa., West Va., and Va. Clients in Regions 2 and 4 are about equal in number—Region 2 comprising the North Atlantic sector—N.J., N.Y., Puerto Rico, Virgin Islands, MD.—and Region 4 comprising the South Atlantic sector—Ala., Fla., Ga., Ky., Miss., N.C., S.C., and Tenn. All clients from Region 9 were located in California.

## Location of Clientele in the State of Michigan:
## Maps 1, 2 and 3

The majority of clients in the State of Michigan are clustered in the southeastern corridor of the state (Ann Arbor, Detroit and Lansing/East Lansing). There is a close correlation between the location of most of the clients and the location of the majority of the elderly residents in the state.

### Non-University Institutions: Table 3

Table 3 displays data on clientele from non-university settings. The data show that after University of Michigan and Institute of Gerontology clients, the third largest group of clients were the private citizens. This group sought information for personal use. Their questions most often concerned in descending order of frequency, the management and relocation of aging parents; questions on retirement, housing and finance; on consumer education; sources of employment after retirement and services and programs available to the aged.

*Business Groups*: The fourth largest group in the non-university category were business groups. In order of priority, clients from the business community requested current demographic information concerning economic, social and population characteristics, followed by mandatory retirement im-

TABLE 2

Sources of Reference Questions Answered 1974-1979

| Clientele Location | Total Number | % of Total |
|---|---|---|
| Univ. of Mich. Students | 200 | 23.8 |
| Institute of Gerontology Staff | 168 | 20.0 |
| Out of State | 151 | 18.4 |
| Detroit Metropolitan | 95 | 11.3 |
| Univ. of Mich. Faculty | 83 | 9.9 |
| Ann Arbor (greater) | 75 | 9.0 |
| Other cities in Michigan | 59 | 6.6 |
| Foreign | 9 | 1.0 |
| | 840 | 100% |

FIGURE 2

DISTRIBUTION OF CLIENTELE BY REGIONS*

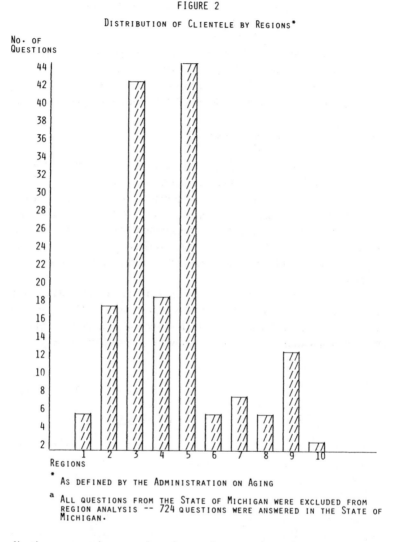

No. OF
QUESTIONS

REGIONS

\* AS DEFINED BY THE ADMINISTRATION ON AGING

a ALL QUESTIONS FROM THE STATE OF MICHIGAN WERE EXCLUDED FROM REGION ANALYSIS -- 724 QUESTIONS WERE ANSWERED IN THE STATE OF MICHIGAN.

plications, pre-retirement plans for employees and psycho-motor skills and mental functioning in old age. The business community was represented by banks, industrial corporations, consulting firms working on behalf of the aged or managing some form of age related service and reporters from the news media.

*Health Related*: There was a cluster of health and care-related establishments: These were clinics, hospitals, day care centers and nursing homes. Clients from these establishments looked for information spanning appropriate physical exercise for the elderly, health-screening techniques, communication disorders, meaningful activities in an institutional setting, training for paraprofessional staff, cost of care for the aged versus the young; and types of memory loss.

*Schools and Churches*: Clients from public school systems and churches made up the smallest category. Teachers and staff from public school systems requested information on appropriate curriculum material in the areas of at-

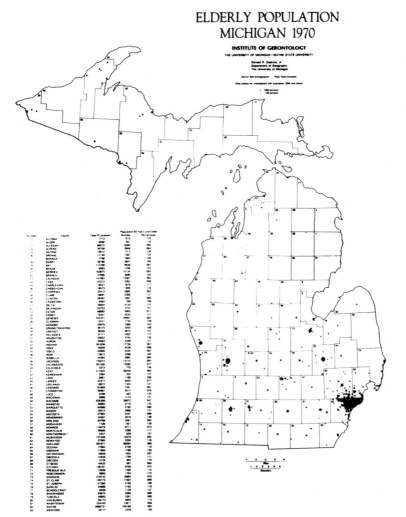

ELDERLY POPULATION
MICHIGAN 1970

INSTITUTE OF GERONTOLOGY

## MAP 2

MICHIGAN - Location of Educational
Institutions

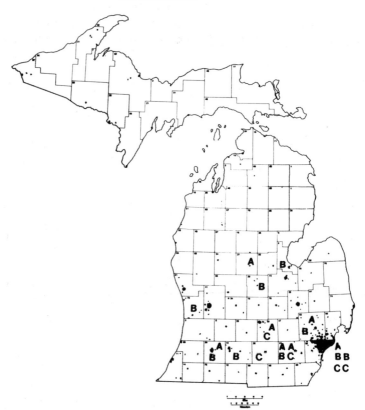

Legend:

```
Universities        A
Colleges            B
Community Colleges  C
```

titudes of children towards old age, on old age as represented in children's literature, and on intergenerational programs and activities.

The clients from churches were concerned primarily with the housing need of older congregational members—and with housing planning and design for the aged. Ministers sought to develop communication skills with aged persons in their congregations.

## Analysis of the Subject of Questions

Information requested by clients in each of the five years studied fell into 18 subject categories. These categories paralleled the social practices
groupings as they are defined by the AOA. (See Figure 3.)
What was of significance in the five year period, 1974–1979, was that

MAP 3

MICHIGAN - Location of Clientele

Legend:

1 – 6 in descending order
1 = High
6 = Low

TABLE 3

Type of Non-University Institutions Served

| TYPE OF CLIENTELE | 1st | 2nd | 3rd | 4th | 5th | TOTAL |
|---|---|---|---|---|---|---|
| Private Citizens | 4 | 8 | 7 | 7 | 8 | 34 |
| Businesses | 6 | 3 | 5 | 4 | 13 | 31 |
| Organizations (Private & National) | 3 | 7 | 7 | 6 | 7 | 30 |
| State and Local Governments | 6 | 5 | 6 | 2 | 8 | 27 |
| State Office on Aging and AAA | 5 | 4 | 6 | 8 | 3 | 26 |
| Nursing Homes | 2 | 3 | 5 | 7 | 8 | 25 |
| Health-Related Facilities | | 3 | 4 | 6 | 4 | 17 |
| Hospitals | 1 | 3 | 1 | 2 | 4 | 10 |
| K-12 Grade Schools | 2 | 1 | 4 | | 3 | 10 |
| Libraries (all types) | | | 2 | 3 | 3 | 8 |
| Federal Government | | 2 | 1 | 2 | 2 | 7 |
| Churches | 1 | 1 | | | | 2 |

FIGURE 3

Subject of Questions Answered

Every Year 1974-1979

| Core Subjects | Health and Care Aspects of Aging | Social Aspects of Aging |
|---|---|---|
| Bibliography | Health | Minorities |
| Research Instruments | Day Care | Legislation |
| Demography | Nursing Homes | |
| Psychology | Long-Term Care | |
| Economics | Physical Fitness | |
| Housing | Therapy/Rehabilitation | |
| Education | | |
| Programs and Services | | |

following the group of core subjects, the remaining questions related to some aspect of health care and social aspects of aging.

Figure 4 shows in 1976 through 1979 the new subject areas show a marked emphasis in the direction of the humanities: i.e., arts, anthropology and journalism. Other new concerns were age discrimination and employment of the older worker and the development of hospice concept in the United States. In addition, another major new concern was in studies of aging internationally—this included family structure, care management, the role of the aged, and attitudes towards the aged in other cultures.

## Degree of Subject Interlocking: Table 4

A table was constructed based on the results of a random sample using 10 percent of the number of questions answered for each year. The data show that social practice and social behavior have the greatest incidence of interlocking. (See Figure 5.)

### FIGURE 4

#### Subject of Questions Answered

| | YEAR 1 | YEAR 2 | YEAR 3 | YEAR 4 | YEAR 5 |
|---|---|---|---|---|---|
| Aging - General | X | X | X | X | X |
| Anthropology | | | | X | X |
| Arts | | | X | X | X |
| Bibliographic | X | X | X | X | X |
| Biology | | | X | X | X |
| Communication Disorders | | X | X | X | X |
| Day Care | X | X | X | X | X |
| Demographic | X | X | X | X | X |
| Drugs | | | X | X | X |
| Economics | X | X | X | X | X |
| Education | X | X | X | X | X |
| Employment | X | | X | X | X |
| Funding | | X | | X | |
| Geriatrics | X | | X | X | X |
| Health (all aspects) | X | X | X | X | X |
| Hospice | | X | | X | X |
| Housing | X | X | X | X | X |
| International Aging | | | X | X | X |
| Journalism | | | | X | X |
| Legal | | X | X | X | X |
| Legislation | X | X | X | X | X |
| Long-Term Care | X | X | X | X | X |
| Media | X | X | | | |
| Minorities | X | X | X | X | X |
| Nursing Homes | X | X | X | X | X |
| Nutrition | X | | X | X | X |
| Physical Fitness | X | X | X | X | X |
| Politics of Aging | | | X | X | X |
| Prisons | | X | X | X | X |
| Psychology | X | X | X | X | X |
| Recreation/Leisure | X | | X | | |
| Religion | | X | X | X | X |
| Research Instruments | X | X | X | X | X |
| Retirement | X | X | X | X | X |
| Services and Programs | X | X | X | X | X |
| Therapy/Rehabilitation | X | X | X | X | X |
| Transportation | | X | X | X | |
| Women | X | X | X | X | X |

X = Questions answered on subject.

TABLE 4

Degree of Subject Interlocking of Questions Answered

| Major Subject Areas | 1st | 2nd | 3rd | 4th | 5th | TOTAL |
|---|---|---|---|---|---|---|
| Total Number of Questions | 118 | 129 | 169 | 184 | 240 | 840 |
| | | | | | | |
| Social Practice | 5 | 4 | 5 | 8 | 12 | 39 |
| Social Behavioral | 1 | 3 | 4 | 2 | 3 | 13 |
| Social Practice & Social Behavioral | 2 | 3 | 3 | 3 | 5 | 16 |
| Social Practice & Bio-Medical | 3 | 2 | 4 | 2 | 2 | 13 |
| Social Behavioral & Bio-Medical | | | | 2 | | 2 |
| 3-part Combination | | | 1 | 1 | 1 | 2 | 5 |
| | | | | | | |
| 10% of Total Each Year | 11 | 13 | 17 | 18 | 24 | 83 |

FIGURE 5

Examples of Subject Interlocking

| Example | 1<br>Drugs | 2<br>Nutrition | 3<br>Women |
|---|---|---|---|
| Social Practice | Patient Education<br>Use and Misuse<br>Use of Generic vs.<br>    Trade Name<br>Media and Advertising | Cultural Aspects<br>Programs<br>Food Stamp Legislation<br>Congregate Meals | Remarriage<br>Employment<br>Soc. Sec.<br>    Differences<br>Income<br>Widow Networks<br>Grandparents |
| Social Behavior | Attitudes Towards<br>    Drugs<br>Compliance<br>Use for Depression | Malnutrition and<br>    Intellectual<br>    Functioning<br>Rejection of Food | Emotional<br>    Support<br>Role Changes<br>Self-Image<br>Attitudes &<br>    Values<br>Life Satisfac-<br>    tion<br>Depression |
| Bio. Medical | Drug Combination<br>    Side Effects<br>Treatment<br>Pharmacology | Diet<br>Calorie Intake<br>Metabolism | Menopause;<br>    Treatment<br>Estrogen<br>    Therapy<br>Chronic<br>    Disease/<br>    Treatment |

*Note:   All questions on Social Practice and Social Behavior were answered by
the Institute of Gerontology Library; and those on Bio. Medical were
referred to the Medical Library.

Since the field of Gerontology is multi-disciplinary by its very nature, it follows that the questions would reflect this structure. As a result, questions often span three or four disciplines before a satisfactory answer can be found. In a number of cases, where manual searches fail to yield sufficient information, the next phase in the search process involved the use of computer searches. Since the information in aging is so widely dispersed a variety of data bases were used.

*Summary*: The data show an extensive staff communication with clients who resided within the university milieu as well as those in the community. This diversity of clientele indicates that persons in the community expected the Institute of Gerontology Library staff to respond to research and lay requests. Similarly, there were indications that the scope of material selected should accommodate three groups of users: (1) the researchers, (2) the practitioners, and (3) the elderly themselves. Since there is an horizontal dimension to material on the subject of aging, liaison with the university departmental libraries such as public health, nursing, social work and medicine are important. Communication and cooperation with the latter departments is vital in order that unnecessary duplication be avoided. Finally, since all documents required for answering reference questions were not housed in the Institute of Gerontology Library, activities were undertaken to locate appropriate documents through the use of a number of national data bases.

# INTEGRATING INFORMATION TECHNOLOGY IN GERONTOLOGY: THE ANDRUS GERONTOLOGICAL INFORMATION CENTER

Margaret Kronauer Longo
Stewart R. Greathouse
Jean E. Mueller

ABSTRACT. Discusses the need for good information in gerontology, the manner in which the Andrus Gerontology Center is contributing to that literature, and the role of the Andrus Gerontological Information Center in accessing, collecting, utilizing, applying and disseminating gerontology's literature. Addresses the shape of the gerontology literature, the way that influences access to the literature, and the indispensable role of online computerized bibliographic databases in facilitating that access. Specific roles, components and services of the Andrus Gerontological Information Center discussed include: the AGEX database, the Dissemination Project/Document Delivery Service, the Research Library, the Computerized Literature Search Service, cross database searching, bibliometric studies, collegial networks, the gerontological information network—GERONET, and future roles of the Andrus Gerontological Information Center.

## Introduction: The Need

One of the newest growth industries in the U.S.—one with impact on just about every facet of American life—is the population of people over 65. At the turn of the century, four out of every hundred persons living in the U.S. were 65 years old or more. Today, more than ten out of every hundred are in that age group. And in the year 2030—just about 50 years from now—as many as one out of every five people will be over 65. At that time the post-World War II baby boom generation reaches 65.

Good information is badly needed for and about the graying of America. We need to know more about the social, behavioral, and biological processes of aging. The information is needed for management and decision-making in all areas of life—housing, health, education, recreation, finances, and communication, to name but a few.[1]

---

Margaret Kronauer Longo is Information Specialist, Stewart R. Greathouse is Information Scientist, and Jean E. Mueller is Chief Librarian at USC Andrus Gerontological Information Center, Los Angeles, CA 90089.

*Meeting the Need: Research, Training and Policy Analysis at the
Andrus Gerontology Center*

The Ethel Percy Andrus Gerontology Center is one of a few institutions in the nation commited to improving the quality of life in later years. Established in 1964, it creates a special environment for research, education and model service in the area of human development and aging. Today, the Center is a leader in fostering both a multidisciplinary and an interdisciplinary approach to the issues and problems related to aging. The goals of the Center are:

— To provide a national leadership in gerontology through programs of excellence in research, education, and model community service to enhance the quality of life for older adults.
— To conduct and support outstanding multidisciplinary basic and community based research in aging.
— To train competent investigators and professionals in aging through degree and non-degree programs of education.
— To bridge the gap between gerontological theory and practice through programs of continuing education and technical assistance.
— To build closer relationships between gerontologists at the University of Southern California and those in other institutions.
— To develop a more efficient collection and exchange of information on research and practice in aging.
— To develop a means for more effective evaluation, utilization, and dissemination of research findings for professional and lay audiences.

The research personnel and faculty at the Center represent a wide variety of disciplines, including psychology, sociology, biology, urban planning, political science, education, public administration, economics, architecture, anthropology, demography, social work and library and information science and management. The Andrus Gerontology's three major operational divisions, the Research Institute, the Leonard Davis School of Gerontology and the Institute for Program and Policy Development, are devoted to accomplishing the objectives enumerated above and the activities of each are described below.

*The Research Institute*

The Gerontology Research Institute consists of seven research laboratories. The research performed at the Institute centers on issues and problems in the areas of neurobiology, developmental psychology and psychophysiology, environmental studies, exercise physiology, social policy, social organization and behavior, and education and aging.

Current research projects include the following:

— Successful aging
— Housing needs and satisfactions of the elderly
— Generational differences: correlates and consequences
— Age differences in learning and memory
— Biological mechanisms of aging
— Physiological effects of conditioning on older persons
— EEG and evoked potential biofeedback in the aged
— Age changes in intelligence and personality during maturity and old age
— Environmental complexity and cognitive functioning through adulthood
— A comparative study of health, retirement and housing among the minority elderly
— Work options for older workers
— Community analysis techniques: making them available to the aging network
— Alternative designs for comprehensive delivery to elderly through case service coordination and advocacy
— Intergenerational housing

Research training is also conducted under the auspices of the Institute. Approximately 65 students are enrolled in doctoral programs in the several disciplines.

## *The Leonard Davis School of Gerontology*

The Leonard Davis School of Gerontology provides professional and preprofessional education in the areas of gerontological studies. The curriculum of the School is designed to promote two basic levels of expertise in aging: (1) Increased knowledge of the biological, psychological, and social processes of aging, and (2) professional skills for dealing with the problems which result from these processes.

The Davis School offers three education programs. The baccalaureate program leads to the award of the Bachelor of Science in Gerontology. The Master of Science in Gerontology is designed to produce professionals and retrain established professionals in the emerging field of aging. The certificate program enables working professionals and paraprofessionals to broaden their knowledge of the field.

*Institute for Program and Policy Development*

The role of the Institute for Program and Policy Development is to build a bridge between applied research and policy application. It:

— Develops models for delivering services that have a nationwide applicability
— Facilitates the professional development of scholars and practitioners through participation in projects
— Disseminates the results of its research and model projects through publications
— Provides technical assistance to community groups, agencies, government entities and the private sector
— Addresses major policy issues and conducts policy relevant research

The recently established National Policy Center on Employment and Retirement is part of the Institute for Program and Policy Development. Its specific purpose is to provide leadership in the analysis and development of policies and programs directed toward the labor force participation and labor force exit of older workers. Also a part of the Institute for Program and Policy Development is the joint UCLA-USC Andrus Center Long Term Care Model Project sponsored by the U.S. Administration on Aging.

*Meeting the Need: Information Collection, Utilization, Application and Dissemination at the Andrus Gerontological Information Center*

One of the major limitations on past scientific research in aging, and its application, has been the failure to plan and implement a systematic and accessible information system which would maximize the utilization of research output. In response to this need for information, the Andrus Gerontological Information Center (AGIC) has established a set of complementary components and services to meet the needs of the research, training and policy analysis activities of the Andrus Gerontology Center. As the AGIC has grown and developed, it has also provided a leadership role within the gerontological information community, as well as served as a national resource for research information in gerontology serving the specific and varied information needs of students, researchers, faculty, business people, policy analysts, decision makers, legislators and the public.

The three components and services of the AGIC include: the Research Library, the Andrus Gerontology Center Dissemination Project/Document

Delivery Service, and the Andrus Gerontological Exchange (AGEX) database and Computerized Information Service.

## Research Library

The Research Library collects and analyzes information on the social, psychological, biological and health aspects of aging. Materials include books, monographs, technical reports government documents and an extensive collection of U.S. doctoral dissertations on life span development and aging; over 100 journal and newsletter titles complete the collection.

## Dissemination Project/Document Delivery Service

The Dissemination Project collects and analyzes materials produced or authored by all personnel and divisions of AGIC's parent organization, the Andrus Gerontology Center, since 1965. Included in the collection are journal articles, monographs, conference papers, final reports of grants, position papers, divisions reports, and bibliographies. The project's Document Delivery Service disseminates hard copy of materials on a cost recovery basis.

## Andrus Gerontological Exchange (AGEX) and the Computerized Information Service

The online, interactive AGEX bibliographic database provides access to all Information Center materials (approximately 10,000 items) with the exception of journals and newsletters. Also included in the database is a special bibliographic file on employment and retirement, developed and supported by the National Policy Center on Employment and Retirement based at the Andrus Center, as well as a Case Coordination and a Health Services Management bibliographic resource file. The database is unique in that each of its citations refers to a document held in the Information Center document collections. Either natural language or controlled vocabulary searching is possible, with descriptive abstracts included for Research Library file records since 1978, and for all Dissemination Project and employment and retirement materials. The AGEX database complements existing online databases, which index journal literature and focuses on providing bibliographic access and control of non-journal materials. The only journal articles indexed by AGEX are those authored by Andrus Center personnel.

The AGIC's Computerized Information Service is the counterpart to the

AGEX database, providing access to the journal literature of databases relevant to gerontology vended by Lockheed, Systems Development Corporation, Bibliographic Retrieval Services, the New York Times and the National Library of Medicine information systems. The Computerized Information Service forms the backbone of the AGIC's information support efforts. Evidence to support this prioritization has been tested and documented, and will be briefly delineated below.

## *The Shape of the Gerontology Literature*

Accessing the literature and other information resources affecting the multidiscipline of gerontology presents a complex and changing scene. It has generally been assumed that the literature of gerontology could be effectively covered with a list of less than 100 journals. This notion was indeed supported by the first U.S. Administration on Aging contracts designed to ascertain the scope and breadth of gerontology's literature. Given the available resources at the time, this appeared to be a reasonable assumption. With the increasing number of online databases, increases in the use of computerized technology for publication production, and systems accessible through local telephone interfaces, the tools to test basic assumptions about the distribution, breadth and scope of at least the journal literature relating to gerontology became available.

The AGIC has taken the position that the journal literature relating to gerontology is widely distributed. AGIC literature searching experience tended to support this point of view. With the aid and incentive of a private information contractor, an opportunity to chart the dimensions of the gerontology journal literature presented itself in 1980. Eighteen separate databases were queried with a complex search strategy designed to isolate not only that information dealing with the elderly "cohort", but the "issues" such as pensions and retirement policy as well. The detailed results of this study will be reported at the 12th International Congress of Gerontology.

The study demonstrated the existence of a core list of perhaps 45 primary journals. This came as no surprise, but the result also identified another 900 journals to be reporting on some aspect of the multidiscipline of gerontology. The results reinforced the cross database searching technique used by the study and developed by the AGIC staff as both valid and useful for ascertaining the full perspective represented in the gerontology literature. The study has important ramifications as to how an information center allocates its resources, since there is a thin diffusion of literature through a net of 1000 journals.

## Andrus Gerontological Information Center's Response

Journal literature is basic to the reporting and dissemination of pure as well as applied research. In comparison to the average 7 year latency period for research to be reported in book form, the period for the same research to be reported in a journal is approximately 2½ years. Clearly, to effectively support teaching, research and policy analysis, priority has been given to the acquisition of journal literature as well as supporting access to that literature through computerized literature searching. Not only has cross database searching provided an index to the journals subscribed to by the AGIC, but it identifies other relevant literature and data as well.

As fiscal criteria for the evaluation of online effectiveness, to subscribe to the 4 printed indexes most often required for identification of the gerontological literature would cost $2500 per year. Of course, online searching allows access to those 4 indexes plus many additional indexes, including one particularly valuable government index, the National Institute of Mental Health Database (NCMH), not available in print copy. In addition, the flexibility of computer searching of machine readable indexes allows greater breadth or specificity of retrieval on any given topic.

### Databases Utilized by the AGIC

Databases searched most often in a cross database mode by the AGIC for gerontological literature include:

Federal information resource databases

ASI American Statistical Index
CIS Congressional Information Service
Fed. Reg. Federal Register Congressional Information Service
Congressional Record, comprehensive index for bills, resolutions, amendments, committee reports, public laws and speeches; allows legislative tracing of testimony and bill history.
Labordoc International Labour Organization, covers industrial policy, journals and monographs related to labor or economic issues.
USGPO Monthly Catalog of Documents from the Govt. Printing Office
NTIS National Technical Information Service
Final and technical reports from government sponsored research
PAIS Public Affairs Information Service
SCAN National Clearinghouse on Aging, AoA

SSIE Smithsonian Science Information Exchange
Current Government research in progress and newly funded projects

General Databases

ERIC National Institute of Education
Grants Index
CDI Comprehensive Dissertation Abstracts
Foundation Index
Management Contents
ABI/Inform American Business Institute
Conference Papers Index

Social/Psychological Databases

Psychological Abstracts American Psychological Association
SSCI Social Science Citation Index Institute for Scientific Information
Sociological Abstracts
NIMHC National Institute of Mental Health Clearinghouse

Biological/Health/Medical Databases

Medline National Library of Medicine
Excerpta Medica
Biosis Previews Biosciences Information Service
Agricola National Agricultural Library
MEDOC Monthly government Documents in Health and Science

In the 2½ years that the AGIC staff has been utilizing computerized databases to access gerontological literature, the gap that has been discerned in the reporting of gerontology literature through online computerized databases has been the area of book, monograph, conference paper and "fugitive" literature. It was determined that the development and production of the AGEX database would be key in bridging that information gap.

*Development of the Andrus Gerontological Exchange Database*

The development of AGEX really begins with the establishment of the Andrus Gerontology Research Library, as it was called at its inception in 1965, and with the foresighted decisions made in those early years which facilitated the smooth and rapid development of a computerized database in gerontology.

*Brief history and description of the Research Library*. The Library began very informally with a collection of the Executive Director's personal materials used by students and located in a downstairs office of the building in which the gerontology program (at that time the Rossmoor-Cortese Institute) was then housed. With a funded National Institute of Child Health and Human Development (NICHD) training grant in 1966, and especially with the first Summer Institute on Aging in 1967, the library became more formalized and the holdings increased considerably. In September 1967 the library was a repository for some 150 books and 4 journals, owned either by the Institute or by staff members. A part-time librarian clerk was hired to handle cataloging and charging out of materials on an overnight basis.

The collection was increased in 1969 to 721 monographs and 43 journals. In the early to mid 1970s holdings increased greatly as a result of a seed money grant from the National Library of Medicine (NLM). The NLM support also made it possible to hire a professional librarian who was supported by University funds as well. From 1970 to 1974 monographs increased from 1113 to 5200; journals from 84 to 90.

It was also during this period that all the ongoing procedures and retrospective cataloging records of the library were converted to a machine-readable format, anticipating the day a software package would be created allowing search and retrieval processes to be executed against the file records.

The opportunity for commissioning the computerized natural language search and retrieval software arrived in December 1977. At that time it was determined that the implementation of the Older Americans Act Title IV-C grant for a Dissemination Project within the Andrus Gerontology Center and the goals of the AGIC were intimately linked. The most efficient way to proceed for their mutual facilitation was to develop a joint database, combining procedures of data entry, database building, and computerized subject searching. Because Library cataloging data were already in machine-readable form, completion of the task was streamlined and development proceeded rapidly.

In the fall of 1978, the operationalization of the AGEX database and its computerized natural language search and retrieval processor began. The development of this software, which runs on USC's IBM 370/155 computer, facilitated searches of the database and the creation of bibliographies to be made available to the Andrus Gerontology Center and its public. The overall capability has been utilized by the document delivery aspect of the Dissemination Project to maintain inventory as well as to create document awareness bibliographies and selective notices of availability for targeted potential audiences. The database and retrieval processor were successfully demonstrated at the meetings of the Gerontological Society held in Dallas,

November 1978. About 200 searches were performed and bibliographies generated for professionals attending the conference. The database has subsequently been discussed and/or demonstrated at five additional national gerontology conferences and has received enthusiastic receptions.

In conjunction with the processor, document input formats and procedures were developed. These permitted online entry of database materials directly into final format using the Andrus Gerontology Center's Varian minicomputer; this, as opposed to a keypunch card operation for creating machine-readable data.

*Growth of AGEX.* The contents of the AGEX database has continued to grow over the years. A major criterion for bibliographic entry of materials into the database has been that the literature not be readily accessible or indexed through other online bibliographic systems. Consequently, the Case Coordination materials acquired to support an AoA grant awarded the Andrus Gerontology Center have been added to the database. Materials consist of largely unreported state and/or local documents and administrative reports. Another criterion has been the utility of a compilation or integration of documents by subject or type. Thus, the entry of citations to doctoral dissertations on aging acquired by the AGIC, documents on Health Services Management, and selected state documents have occurred. Besides the continued development of these specialized resources, the general book/monograph core of the database has been facilitated by a subject profile with a computer-based book jobber. Of course, the entire information community looks forward to the availability of large book databases online. However, until that happens, AGEX is still a unique resource for books in gerontology, as well as for a retrospective coverage of all the aforementioned types of literature not available through other online systems.

*Development of Additional Services, Roles and Functions of the Andrus Gerontological Information Center*

*Bibliometric studies.* One of the analysis functions of the Information Center is to identify gaps and overlaps in the literature. Analytic activities occur as an automatic consequence of utilizing computers for the retrieval of information online. Bibliometrics is the quantitative analysis of the bibliographic and informational features of a body of literature.

Bibliometric analysis, in conjunction with database systems, is an analytic activity capable of characterizing and profiling existent literature. These profiles or overviews produce information about the density of issue coverage, scatter of literature, rate of publication, and changing trends.

Using computerized retrieval systems in conjunction with databases provides a wide analytic window through which research progress and knowledge growth can be viewed and analyzed. The computer is the tool of choice in these situations because of quantum increases in the amount of available literature and, in the case of information relating to the elderly, the diffusion through various disciplines and various government agency reports and projects.

Postings (i.e., the number of citations for specific topics or concepts) provide indications of the shape, content and scatter of specific disciplines provides firm insight into the translation process of research-to-application being discussed in the literature and identifies gaps in the base. These techniques can be harnessed for research, planning, and applications.

*Current awareness updates.* As a means of providing the most up-to-date information, the AGIC can provide current awareness services. These are updates of previous searches, they are added as new literature becomes available. This function results in a comprehensive compilation of literature on primary topics. In this way, searches, which define and review topics, can be stored online and run against updates of the database, augmenting prior search topics. Current awareness services are now part of database vendor systems and are available for the AGEX database as well. They provide a useful cost-effective tool for continuing awareness updates.

*Collegial network facilitation.* Too frequently efforts, particularly those of a new or innovative nature, fail to draw upon what is already known. This body of knowledge consists of both the written literature and the vast amount of information available from collegial networks. Less frequently associated with the information retrieval process is location of colleagues dealing with and attempting to solve the same problems and conducting projects of a similar nature (begun but not yet published).

Access to and awareness of a collegial network and its projects is extremely important. In a study by Nathan Kaplan investigating information seeking behavior of presidential advisors, their prime source of information was colleagues. Defining a collegial network for a multidiscipline such as gerontology is complex process requiring access to existent literature with discrete disciplinary perspectives.

Cross disciplinary bridging is one of the key factors explored within the gerontological context. Successful utilization of each disciplinary perspective and skill is the key and one of the major challenges facing gerontology. Again, access to several different systems (databases), each with a component of specialized information, is essential. Access to and utilization of this technology are the specialty of the AGIC staff. To apply and utilize what is already known without reinventing the wheel has implications to the overall success of gerontology research, training and application.

*The gerontological information network—GERONET.* In 1973, the Andrus Gerontology Center's librarian and the Chief of the Laboratory of Social Policy presented a paper on information resources and needs in gerontology at the Gerontological Society annual meeting in Miami. This presentation acted as a catalyst in bringing together a nucleus group of persons concerned about these information needs, including librarians at other institutions of higher learning. Since then, this interest in gerontological information resources has resulted in the creation of an informal network with the Andrus Gerontological Information Center staff continuing to play a major role. Some of the issues and suggested solutions set forth in "Toward a Comprehensive Information System, a Survey of Problems, Resources and Potential Solutions" by Miller and Cutler in 1976 continue to provide guidelines for this group.

The group has continued to meet at Gerontological Society and Western Gerontological Society annual meetings. 1977 saw the formalization of the group to the educational committee of the Gerontological Society of America. A program was organized and accepted at the 1977 San Francisco meeting. Most recently, the annual Gerontological Librarian's group meeting held in conjunction with the Gerontological Society convention in San Diego in November 1980 addressed several issues including the need for a mechanism to facilitate communication and networking among gerontology libraries and librarians. Though the network has been identified for some time, cooperative efforts have been stymied due to geographic dispersion and fiscal restraints.

The concept and theory of networks has experienced great popularity in recent years because it is a concept concerned with:

> the extent, substance and form of human relationships in a world in which everybody and everything seems interrelated, actually or potentially...(Networking)...seem to have the potential for a better understanding and resolution of thorny problems of improving resource utilization intra- and interagency coordination and information sharing.[2]

Thus, in an era demanding extreme fiscal accountability and efficiency, the network concept has been appealing in terms of gaining the most benefits for the least expenditure of resources. Ironically, some of the same factors that had prevented effective information networking could potentially be alleviated by facilitating such a network.

In anticipation of this discussion, a representative of the California Library Authority for Systems and Services (CLASS) spoke to the group on

RLIN, an online cataloging service, and on Ontyme, an electronic mail service. Her presentation gave us an authoritative base for the subsequent discussions. Applications of Ontyme of special interest to the library community are:

— interlibrary loan communication
— reference and referral
— ready reference—sharing information frequently requested by storing it on a shared file
— communication among members of any number or kind of groups
— intra or inter institutional communication with traveling members of organizations
— planning of joint activities

The AGIC and the NRTA/AARP National Resource Center have taken the initiative to form GERONET utilizing the message switching capability of Ontyme as a technological base to effectively link the gerontological information community. The AGIC encourages anyone interested in GERONET to contact the AGIC staff for further information.

*Other Resources, Projects and Contributions Related to Information in Gerontology at the Andrus Gerontological Information Center*

*Handbook Projects.* Dr. James E. Birren, Executive Director and Dean of the L. Davis School of Gerontology has had a continuing interest in information compilation, retrieval and dissemination. Author of the first *Handbook of Aging and the Individual* (1959), he more recently (1976) was editor-in-chief of three widely acclaimed handbooks on aging: *Handbook of Aging and the Social Sciences,Handbook of the Psychology of Aging* and *Handbook of the Biology of Aging.* A fourth handbook, the *Handbook of Mental Health and Aging* was published in 1980.

*Bibliographies.* An activity connected with the handbook projects has been to provide bibliographies to all chapter authors, which has resulted in a massive keysort database of over 60,000 citations on aging. These include the majority of references from Nathan Shock's bibliography on current publications in geriatrics and gerontology published in the *Journal of Gerontology.* The keysort files have subsequently been used as a source file for nine technical bibliographies published by the Andrus Center.

*Technical Bibliographies on Mental Health and Aging.* 1981 saw the completion of the NIMH sponsored grant ''Technical Bibliographies on Mental Health and Aging''. The series of five bibliographies include: Depression, Self-Destructive Behavior and Aging, Neurobiology of Aging, Psychopharmacology and Aging, Stress and Aging and Competence Over the Adult Years. Extensive computerized literature searching provided the address to the knowledge base for the project.

*Doctoral Dissertation Bibliography.* ''A Bibliography of Doctoral Dissertations on Aging from American Institutions of Higher Learning'' is a publication compiled by two librarians of the AGIC, and has been published annually in the *Journal of Gerontology* since 1971. This unique resource of 2000+ citations is currently being indexed for a proposed cumulation to occur in 1984. These also compose part of the online AGEX database.

*Library Collection Publication.* The AGIC's research library collection holdings were published by G.K. Hall of Boston in 1974. An updated version of this publication is planned for the future.

## The Future

### Information Analysis and the Creation of a Knowledge Base

One of the key projects for the AGIC is to begin to synthesize and reduce these information packages into a manageable dimension for access by student, faculty, researchers, decision-makers and the community. Thus, a key function for the Information Center is information analysis. Rees (1974) characterizes an information analysis center as: a formally structured organization for the purpose of acquiring, selecting, storing, retrieving, evaluating, analyzing and synthesizing a body of information or data in a clearly defined field or special mission with the intent of compiling, digesting, repackaging or presenting pertinent information or data. The information is utilized for:

1. conduction of science
2. effective generation of technology and its applications
3. decisionmaking and policy formulation
4. enlightenment of the general public through education and public information
5. contribution to the creation of a knowledge base

The Andrus Gerontological Information Center has begun to contribute to the development of a knowledge base through analysis, editing, evaluation and synthesis of information on topics and issues of primary interest in gerontology.

## Summary of the Andrus Gerontological Information Center as an Information Resource

The Andrus Gerontological Information Center is:

— AGEX (Andrus Gerontological Exchange)
— The Dissemination Project/Document Delivery Service
— Access to online, computerized, bibliographic databases for literature searches

### AGEX Database Custom Searches

| How to Utilize | Cost | How Long |
|---|---|---|
| Write or phone for search request form. Pre-payment required with completed form. | minimum $10 | 2–3 weeks |

### Other Database Custom Searches

| How to Utilize | Cost | How Long |
|---|---|---|
| Write or phone for search form. $25 deposit required with completed form. | minimum $25 service charge, plus computer connect, tele-communications output and mailing costs | 2–3 weeks |

### Dissemination Project Document Availability Lists

| How to Utilize | Cost | How Long |
|---|---|---|
| Write or phone. | $5 (applied to minimum $5 purchase | 2–3 weeks |

Other services include:

— consulting services for special information projects in gerontology and database development are available
— consulting services for becoming a GERONET member

Contact:

Andrus Gerontological Information Center
University of Southern California
University Park
Los Angeles, California 90089–0191

## FOOTNOTES

1. Anonymous. "Wanted: Information About and For the Aging. An Interview With Robert N. Butler, M.D., Director of the National Institute on Aging". *Bulletin of the American Society for Information Science*, 1978, 5(1), p. 14.

2. Rees, A. M. "Functional Integration of Technical Libraries, Information Centers and Information Analysis Centers." In: Rees, A. M. *Contemporary Problems in Technical Library and Information Center Management: A State-of-the-Art*. Washington, D.C.: American Society for Information Science, 1974, p. 119.

3. Sarason, S. and E. Lorentz. *The Challenge of the Resource Exchange Network*. San Francisco: Jossey Bass, 1979, p. 38.

# THE NATIONAL GERONTOLOGY RESOURCE CENTER: THE PUBLIC PERSPECTIVE

Paula M. Lovas

## A Brief History and Introduction

The National Gerontology Resource Center is supported and funded by the National Retired Teachers Association-American Association of Retired Persons (NRTA-AARP), a membership organization of 12 million persons age 55 and over, and is located at their headquarters building in Washington, D.C. It was founded as the Associations' library in the mid-1960s, concomitant with two major developments which occurred at the Associations at approximately the same time: the establishment of their innovative and highly successful Institute of Lifetime Learning program, which offered continuing education opportunities to retired persons, primarily through daytime courses in the arts and the humanities; and the development of a Washington-based NRTA-AARP national affairs office designed to strengthen and promote the interests of older Americans through input into the legislative process. From the beginning, the library was designated as a research and technical, rather than a recreational, collection; this orientation reflected the background of the NRTA-AARP founder and first president, Dr. Ethel Percy Andrus, who as a retired California high school principal, devoted great time and energy to early efforts to educate the public, legislators, and the elderly themselves about the continuing potential for creativity and productivity in later life. Editorials written by Dr. Andrus in the early years of NRTA and AARP document her pioneering efforts to overcome stereotypes of the elderly as lonely, senile, withdrawn, and unable to contribute to society. Beginning in the 1950s, her continuing calls for an end to mandatory retirement stressed the productive capabilities of older persons, and their continuing right and need to contribute to society. Though there is little written record, the establishment of a gerontological library collection at NRTA-AARP was most probably intended to support the

Paula M. Lovas is Head, National Gerontology Resource Center, NRTA-AARP, 1909 K Street, N.W., Washington, D.C. 20049.

presentation of a factual and positive view of the elderly as active, committed and contributing members of society.

Through the early 1970s, the library continued to serve primarily as a resource for NRTA-AARP staff. In the mid-1970s its focus changed and its mandate was enlarged, emphasizing the provision of information service to the public, to the extent that this was feasible considering the inevitable limitations of staff and time. Initial efforts were made to reach out to other institutions within the gerontological community, and from there, to other interested public organizations, government agencies, and researchers. In 1978, the title "Library" was dropped, and the name National Gerontology Resource Center was adopted, to reflect this growing commitment to service to the public.

At the present time, the National Gerontology Resource Center is operated as a public educational service of NRTA-AARP. It has a reference staff of 5 persons and a technical staff of 4. It is prepared to provide telephone consultation and reference service, and to respond to information requests of a specific nature. It is open for use as a library and reference facility by researchers, students and the general public. It houses one of the largest collection of materials in social gerontology, approximately 9,000 volumes, plus 600 journal and newsletter subscriptions.

By making these resources available to the public, it is dedicated to furthering and promoting knowledge about aging and the older population.

One additional feature of the Resource Center is an Information Analyst position designed to prepare literature reviews or conduct research studies, on an ad hoc basis, on topics of particular interest to the Associations. Recent information analysis activities have included a review of the literature on retirement communities in an effort to understand future trends in retirement communities as a housing choice for older persons; a study of state teacher retirement systems; an extensive study of work options or alternative work patterns which are, or may in the future, be used by older workers as an alternative to full withdrawal from the work force; and the preparation of materials for use at the 1981 White House Conference on Aging. These projects are enumerated here, preceding a fuller description of the library collection, as an effort to familiarize the reader with the wide variety of issues and concerns which fall under the purview of a gerontological library collection.

## Collection Development

Three major factors have been influential in determining the nature and characteristics of the National Gerontology Resource Center collection:

1. For purposes of collection policy, the term "social gerontology" has

been interpreted in its broadest sense; that is, subjects and materials which in other circumstances might be considered peripheral to gerontology have generally been included, rather than excluded.

2. An effort has been made to build a *comprehensive*, rather than highly selective, library collection. The possibility of doing so was greatly aided by a fortuitous set of circumstances. First, the fact that gerontology as a field was relatively young and the literature base, in the beginning, was relatively small, made it fairly easy to ensure that most publications were acquired. Second, the establishment of the library in the mid-1960s coincided with two major developments in the field of aging: the passage of Medicare legislation in 1965, as well as enactment of the Older Americans Act, also in 1965. Since both events prompted an increase in the number of aging-related studies and reports, it was fortunate that selection and acquisition procedures were already established, and staff were able to monitor and acquire appropriate items. The physical location of the library in Washington, DC, where the majority of federal, congressional and consultant reports originate, has also been of immeasurable help in pursuing a comprehensive acquisitions policy.

Third, and perhaps most significantly, up to the present time both budget and space have been sufficient to allow for development of a comprehensive collection (though admittedly not without determined efforts on the part of current and past librarians); realistically, however, it is clear that there are now increasing constraints in both the areas of budget and space, and the feasibility of trying to maintain a comprehensive gerontology collection is currently being questioned by others as well as myself. While the outcome of this discussion has yet to be determined, it is almost certain to have an impact on the future direction of the Resource Center library collection: either by limiting the definition of subject areas or items considered appropiate for the collection or, more hopefully, by prompting exploration of more efficient and effective ways of acquiring, processing and storing materials. Two trends which may help to support the latter choice are the decreasing costs of automation, with the attendant possibilities for increased networking; and the development of the SCAN system under the sponsorship of the U.S. Administration on Aging, which when fully implemented should provide extensive indexing of documents stored on microfiche.

The Resource Center has participated from the beginning as a repository library in the SCAN system. It automatically receives microfiche copies of all documents included in the system, and has microform reader/printers available for reproducing the documents in hard copy.

3. Finally, as a state-of-the-art resource collection, considerable staff time has been devoted both by reference and acquisitions staff to the building and incorporation of non-traditional resource files which are perhaps the hallmark of a special library. Extensive files have been constructed of per-

sonal contacts at government agencies, public and private organizations, universities, and the media. Users of the Resource Center, frequently researchers and writers, in turn often become resource contacts for future inquiries. Where possible, inventories of aging-related programs and services have been compiled or purchased, and frequent reference is made to these in responding to information requests. Extensive pamphlet files, using subject headings narrower than those in the card catalog, are assiduously compiled from the viewpoint that they should present an overview of, as well as the latest developments on, a topic; they are continually reviewed for content and currency. Because there are no indexes specifically devoted to the gerontological literature, these files often contain recent newspaper clippings, journal articles, and conference papers, and Resource Center users are frequently referred to these files before proceeding on to the book or report literature.

## Scope and Characteristics of the Collection

Despite personal familiarity with it, efforts to define the subject matter and scope of the Resource Center's gerontological collection constitute a challenging task—and not without reason, for this dilemma reflects the nature of gerontology itself, a field invariably described by its exponents as inter-related, interdisciplinary, and multidisciplinary in nature. For purposes of this discussion, the following definitions and explanation from Robert Atchley capture best the varying efforts to delineate and define gerontology. The passage is from Atchley's book, *The Social Forces in Later Life; an Introduction to Social Gerontology*, where it appears under the heading "Gerontology Defined":

> It is a complex subject, wandering far and wide across the traditional lines of academic study. Yet it never strays from a basic concern with older persons, and with the processes of physical and social aging. Doctors study the illnesses of older people; biologists study the physical changes that aging brings to the cells of the body; psychiatrists study mental illness among older people; psychologists study age changes in sensory perception; economists study the income requirements of older people; architects design special housing for older people; and sociologists study the relationships between older people and their society and culture. Almost every area of study dealing with people or their needs has a branch that deals with older humans. All of these tiny branches of these many fields come together under the name of gerontology—literally, 'the logic of aging.'

There are four related but separate aspects to the study of aging. The biological aspect deals with physical aging—the body's gradual loss of the ability to renew itself. The psychological aspect deals with the sensory processes—perception, motor skills, intelligence, problem-solving ability, understanding, learning processes, drives, and emotions of the aging individual. The biological and psychological changes that occur with advancing age are coupled with the social environment of the individual to produce a third aspect—the behavioral. This aspect of aging deals with the aged person's attitudes, expectancies, motives, self-image, social roles, personality, and psychological adjustment to aging. Finally, the sociological aspect of aging deals with the society in which aging occurs, the influence this society has on aging individuals, and the influence they have on society. The health, income, work, and leisure of older people as these areas relate to their families, friends, voluntary associations, and religious groups, as well as to society in general, the economy, the government, and the community, are all part of the sociology of aging.

These four aspects of aging—biological, psychological, behavioral and sociological—are all interrelated in the life of older people.[1]

Atchley goes on to define social gerontology as follows:

Social gerontology is the subfield of gerontology that deals primarily with the nonphysical aspects of aging. Clark Tibbitts, one of the founders of social gerontology, describes it as 'concerned with the developmental and group behavior of adults following maturation and with the social phenomena which give rise to and arise out of the presence of older people in the population.'[2]

Biological and psychological aspects of aging interest the social gerontologist only insofar as they influence the ways in which the individual and society adapt to each other. Yet because biology and psychology are at the root of the social aspects of aging, social gerontologists must understand as much as they can about these areas.[3]

Traditionally, the Resource Center collection has been described as a "social gerontology" collection, not because it is primarily limited to this subfield, but because the social gerontology literature has tended to predominate the gerontological literature generally, and therefore constitutes the bulk of the National Gerontology Resource Center collection. By Atchley's definition of gerontology, it would be accurate to say that the Resource Center collection is very strong in the psychological, behavioral, and sociological aspects of aging, and fairly strong in the biological aspects of aging. Only one subject area—geriatric medicine, defined as "disease in old age"[4]—has generally been excluded from the collection by intention, because the Resource Center did not serve a user group with experience or research interests in geriatric medicine.

The collection is also limited to English-language materials, primarily those published in the U.S. British monographs and studies are included selectively, and a special effort is made to include all cross-national studies published in English.

It may be useful to highlight at this point certain sociological influences or trends which have had a particular impact on the study of aging, and which are reflected in the Resource Center's library collection. Perhaps the most important of these is *demography* and its effect upon the "demographics of aging." For a description of the stages of later life, and a discussion of the search for a definition of "older person," the reader is again referred to Atchley's *The Social Forces in Later Life*, particularly to the description, based on Tibbitts' work, of three stages of advanced adulthood—middle age, later maturity and old age.[5] While a long tradition has defined the older population as those persons 65 and over, the middle-aged (as precursors to this later stage of life) cannot be ignored. The tremendous growth in the number and proportion of middle-aged and older persons. together with the steadily increasing median age, have combined to focus greater attention on demographics as a special concern in the field of aging. The Resource Center reflects this trend, including in its collection population studies, predictions and forecasts, as well as demographic studies and reports issued by population research institutes and the U.S. Bureau of the Census. The increasing number of four-generation families, the concern of the middle-aged in caring for aged parents, and the emergence of two generations in retirement, are special issues directly attributable to demographic changes.

Another area of concentration is health care: the organization of, demand for, and delivery of health care services, as well as health care policy. The rising costs of medical care, the increasing percentage of health care costs borne directly by the elderly themselves, and the growing numbers of the very old (those 75 and above, who require increased medical attention) all contribute to a high level of interest in the health care literature. Of special interest are publications dealing with alternatives to traditional medical services, such as home health care, social services which can prevent or delay institutionalization, and hospices.

There is an emphasis in the collection on women, for several reasons:

their longer life expectancy (in 1978, among persons 65 and over, there were 146 women per 100 men); rising divorce rates and the emergence of the "displaced homemaker" phenomenon (women with little work experience. few job skills, and the need to earn current, as well as future retirement, income); and the changing roles of women, both married and single, particularly as this affects their entry or re-entry into the labor market. In fact, a special effort is made to collect all publications on the older worker, both from the viewpoint of the worker and the employer: job abilities and performance, preferences for work or for retirement, alternatives to full-time employment, retirement options, effects of the 1978 Age Discrimination in Employment Act, which prohibits mandatory retirement, and retirement planning programs. While the literature in this area is generally sparse, it is expected to increase in the next few years; those currently interested, but unfamiliar with what does exist, are referred to the excellent quarterly journal *Aging and Work* (formerly *Industrial Gerontology*)[6] which presents timely and thorough discussions of the issues mentioned above. The retirement planning publications issued by AIM (Action for Independent Maturity, a division of NRTA-AARP) are also useful for training and public education programs.[7]

Finally, the Resource Center reflects its heritage as the library of a voluntary membership association through its collection of the literature on volunteerism and voluntary participation. Again, the literature in this subject area is relatively sparse, and an effort has been made to acquire all substantive publications relating to volunteer activity. There is also a small archives which contains copies of all testimony and publications issued by NRTA-AARP, as well as indexes to the Associations' major publications, *Modern Maturity* (issued by AARP), *NRTA Journal*, and *Dynamic Maturity* (issued by AIM).

## Historical Collections

The Resource Center includes four special collections of a historical nature, containing a number of items not widely available elsewhere. These are:

1. Complete holdings from the various White House Conferences on Aging (1961, 1971 and 1981), as well as the predecessor "First National Conference on Aging" sponsored by the Federal Security Agency in 1950.
2. Complete holdings of all hearings and reports issued by the U.S.

Senate Special Committee on Aging and its predecessor agency, the Subcommittee on Problems of the Aged and Aging, of the Senate Committee on Labor and Public Welfare.

3. Complete holdings of all hearings and reports issued by the U.S. House Select Committee on Aging; and the aging-related documents issued by the House Committee on Education and Labor, and the Committee on Ways and Means, which handled the majority of aging-related legislation prior to the establishment of the House Select Committee on Aging in 1975.

4. There is a unique 50-book collection called ''Retired Teachers' Reflections,'' which consists of one book from each state recounting the history and experiences of teaching in that state. The series was prepared as a Bicentennial contribution by members of the National Retired Teachers Association; some of the books had a fairly large print run and were sold within their states, while others are single-edition items. The books are largely anecdotal, and while style and quality vary considerably among them, in total they present a fascinating account of U.S. elementary and secondary school teaching in the earlier years of the 20th century.

Materials from the ''Retired Teachers Reflections'' and items in the other special collections which are held in one copy only are not available on interlibrary loan; they are, however, readily available for use at the Resource Center and are mentioned here in an effort to ensure that anyone searching for materials on the history of U.S. aging legislation, or on teaching in the U.S., is familiar with their existence.

### *Services and Publications*

The library collection and telephone reference service previously described are supplemented by the use of automated databases, and the production of several publications. At the present time, computerized bibliographic searching is done primarily as a service for NRTA-AARP staff; a payment mechanism does not exist for public searching, although it is hoped that one may be established in the future. Occasionally, public inquiries on subjects which are known to be of special interest to NRTA-AARP staff members will be searched via computer, with costs absorbed by the Resource Center. Search printouts are generally saved to avoid duplication, and are available for referral. The Lockheed, SDC, BRS, Information Bank and MEDLARS systems are currently accessible; the databases most widely used to date are *Psychological Abstracts, Sociological Abstracts, Congressional Record* and *Federal Register,* ERIC, MEDLINE, and the *Information Bank.*

At present, Interlibrary Loan requests are generated primarily from the Washington, D.C. area, although the Resource Center intends to make its materials as available as possible and not to limit access if other sources are unavailable. Persons who are interested in inquiring about either automated searches or Interlibrary Loan are encouraged to call the Resource Center; if we are not familiar with a facility located in your area which can provide the services needed, search and Interlibrary Loan requests will be considered on an individual basis. The telephone number for search requests is (202) 872-4844; for Interlibrary Loan requests, (202) 872-4961. The Resource Center is open from 9:00 am - 5:00 pm, Monday through Friday, except holidays.

The Resource Center issues the following publications, free on request:

1. *Introductory Readings in Social Gerontology,* 1981, 14pp. An annotated bibliography of 40 basic books covering all aspects of social gerontology.
2. *A Basic Reference Collection for Information Specialists,* March 1980, 8pp. A list of basic reference works in gerontology, including directories, readers' advisory and information sources, bibliographies and statistical publications, useful addresses and mailing lists.
3. *Bi-Monthly Accessions List.* A listing by subject of all items cataloged and added to the Resource Center collection in the previous two months, with full cataloging information. The Resource Center uses the LC classification system.
4. *National Gerontology Resource Center Users' Guide,* 1981, 12pp. A description of the Resource Center's collection, services and policies.

Please address requests for any of the above to:

National Gerontology Resource Center
NRTA-AARP
1909 K St., N.W.
Washington, DC 20016
Attn: Acquisitions

(Persons requesting the *Accessions List* will be sent a sample copy, with a request to reply if they wish to be added to the mailing list for future issues.)

Two other items which are generated for internal use may be of interest to librarians. The *Weekly Journal Contents Service,* similar in concept to *Current Contents,* contains the Contents page of all newly received journals having articles relevant to gerontology. Presently, this is distributed to NRTA-AARP staff, and to a small mailing list of other gerontological libraries. A list of Subject Headings in use at the Resource Center has been compiled using word processing equipment, and is also available for distribution. Person interested in receiving these items are asked to address their requests in care of the author, at the above address.

It is hoped that this description and guide to the National Gerontology Resource Center collection and services will be of assistance to others who are establishing or building gerontological collections, as well as those who seek a source of public information to supplement their own resources. The assistance of Resource Center staff in the provision of information and services described here, as well as in the preparation of this manuscript, are acknowledged by the author with appreciation.

## REFERENCES

1. Atchley, Robert. *The Social Forces in Later Life; an Introduction to Social Gerontology,* 2nd edition, Belmont, CA, Wadsworth Publishing Co., 1977, p. 5.

2. Tibbitts, Clark. "The Future of Research in Social Gerontology," in *Age with a Future,* edited by P. From Hansen, Copenhagen, Munksgaard, 1964, p. 139.

3. Atchley, *op cit,* p. 5.

4. Besdine, Richard W., M.D. "Geriatric Medicine: An Overview," in *Annual Review of Gerontology and Geriatrics,* New York, Springer Publishing Co., Volume 1, 1980, p. 135.

5. Atchley, *op cit,* p. 10.

6. Aging and Work; a Journal on Age, Work and Retirement (formerly Industrial Gerontology). Issued quarterly, Volume 3, 1980; published by The National Council on the Aging, Inc., Washington, D.C. Subscription $30/yr.

7. *Looking Ahead: How to Plan Your Successful Retirement,* Washington, D.C., Action for Independent Maturity, 1980, 92pp., $9.95.

# INFORMATION TRANSFER
# IN GERONTOLOGY AND HEALTH:
# A CENTRALIZED AND A DECENTRALIZED
# MODEL

Marta L. Dosa

## Information, the Abundant and Elusive Resource

Theodore Caplow (1975) observed that "a greatly improved society might be within our present grasp if projects of social improvement were undertaken in a more rational way...we already have most of the theoretical knowledge required..." (p. vii). In and attempt to cope with the widely perceived need to manage and use knowledge more efficiently, our society has produced an immense apparatus of sophisticated information systems in both the public and the private sectors. New information needs, created by demographic, social and economic trends, have been recognized by federal legislation as well as by the information marketplace. "More and more bills are being introduced, and more and more laws are being enacted which contain—in whole or in part—mandates for new computer systems or data bases, [and] directives for collecting or disseminating information" (U.S. Congress.House, 1979).

Laws requiring the creation of information clearinghouses and centers have been concerned with a wide range of issues, for example, aging, community mental health centers, consumer product safety, Medicare-Medicaid, and so on. Of special relevance to this symposium is the National Rural In-

Marta L. Dosa, Ph.D., is Professor is the School of Information Studies Syracuse University, Syracuse, NY 13210. This paper was presented at the Symposium on Building Linkages Between the Researcher and the rural Practitioner in the Field of Aging, North Country Center of Gerontology, Saranac Lake, N.Y., September 13–14, 1979. The activities described were in part supported by Administration on Aging Grant 90–A–1054 under Title IV-C of the Older Americans Act and by the National Library of Medicine through NIH Grant LM 02800. The opinions expressed in this paper are those of the author.

*53*

formation Clearinghouse in the Department of Commerce providing information services on human development and economic programs needed in counties, towns, villages and sparsely inhabited rural areas (Vinson and Chewning, 1978).

Statistical data relevant to a wide range of human concerns are also available from governmental and private sources in more abundance than most practitioners recognize. In the health sector alone, massive collection, analysis and publication of statistics were mandated by the Health Services Research, Health Statistics, and Health Care Technology Act of 1978 that established the Cooperative Health Statistics System. In Fiscal Year 1977, the Public Health Service alone administered 153 data collection projects. The U.S. Office of Technology Assessment (1979) identified the problems connected with these data collection efforts as fragmentation; burden on institutions that have to report data; inefficient use and an inability to collect data that cut across federal agency jurisdictions (p. 3).

In the field of aging, the National Clearinghouse on Aging, through its Sevice Center for Aging Information (SCAN) operates a computer-based information storage and retrieval system and specialized resource centers. A National Archive of Computerized Data on Aging has also been funded by AoA at the University of Michigan. In addition, private companies are marketing information in print, microform, on film, tape and disc Bibliographic data bases cover more and more subjects in the social science and the human services field. It is now virtually impossible to have an over view of all the potential information sources relevant to any one proble or any one individual's work (Figure 1). Some of these sources are dynam and use intensive methods to make potential consumers aware of t availability of information while others are ''invisible'', and must be track down by the end user or an information intermediary.

Can the abundance of this information production be sifted and cha neled to local communities in some relevant way? Two closely related prol lems must be faced by gerontologists who want to build linkages betwee new insights gained by research and the work-related needs of service pro viders. One is the problem of the practitioner and policy maker who want to base service-related decisions on information about client groups, past experience and cases, research-generated data and available alternatives of approach and outcome. The other, even more complex issue relates to our inadequate understanding of the information needs of elderly people. We must plan for information systems that will enable the service providers to assist, with the right kind of information, the choices older people must make in their physically and economically often restricted lives. But we also must

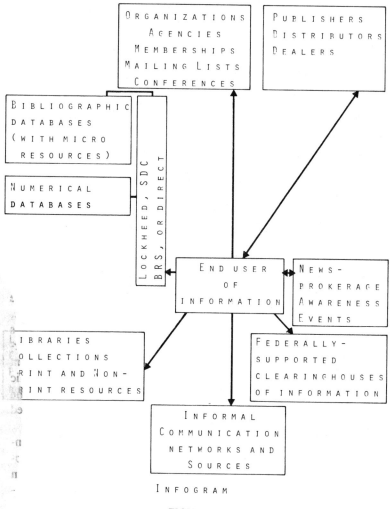

FIGURE 1

find a way to reach the elderly who do not seek services and who, by having access to information, can better cope with problems, enjoy their lives, and enrich others. These concerns are interrelated because our society tends to build helping systems for those situations where illness, poverty and isolation have already taken their toll, and has been known to ignore the need for basic information that would prevent crises and enhance the overall quality of life. We need simultaneously professional work-related information and everyday coping and enriching information (Figure 2).

Decisions in gerontological practice are not different from decisions in any other sector. It has often been said that decisions are only as good as the information on which they are based. Public policies are being increasingly aimed at the development of large-scale information systems. In 1976, the National Commission on Libraries and Information Science emphasized that a national information policy should "encourage access to information and information systems and strengthen the private sector so that, through competition, innovation can be encouraged" (U.S. National Commission on Libraries and Information Science, 1976, p. 202). Although there is no shortage of innovative technologies and services, many decisions are still being made in the absence of valid data. In reference to human services Holland (1976), following and examination of information utilization systems, concluded that "in most organizations, the collection and use of information is basically an informal process and decision making is far from routine or rational . . . ." (p. 33). Nor have the policy making bodies whose decisions affect the lives of the elderly a firmer foundation of knowledge. Recently the General Accounting Office warned:

> To design and plan for the delivery of services to older persons, society, the Congress, and the executive branch need information on their well-being, the factors that make a difference in their lives, and the impact of services on them. Currently, this information is spread piecemeal through Federal, State, local and private agencies. The result: Federal agencies have not evaluated the combined effect of these services, and in the absence of such information, assessing the impact of various laws on the lives of older people is difficult (U.S. General Accounting Office, 1979, p. ii).

There is substantial evidence in the literature that, although an abundance of information is available in our society, the quality, timeliness and relevance of information have not improved. In this sense, researchers and practitioners share a common concern: the need for better knowledge utilization.

*Factors that Heighten Information Needs*

Recent changes in our society created an upsurge in research, public policies and programs of national scope for the elderly. Some of these changes (new trends, relationships, regulations, technologies, etc.), while

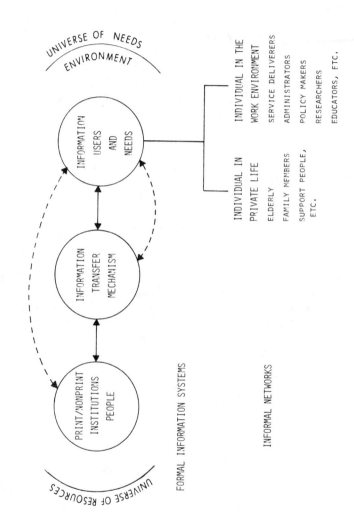

UNIVERSE OF NEEDS
ENVIRONMENT

INFORMATION
USERS
AND
NEEDS

INFORMATION
TRANSFER
MECHANISM

PRINT/NONPRINT
INSTITUTIONS
PEOPLE

UNIVERSE OF RESOURCES

FORMAL INFORMATION SYSTEMS

INFORMAL NETWORKS

INDIVIDUAL IN THE
WORK ENVIRONMENT
SERVICE DELIVERERS
ADMINISTRATORS
POLICY MAKERS
RESEARCHERS
EDUCATORS, ETC.

INDIVIDUAL IN
PRIVATE LIFE
ELDERLY
FAMILY MEMBERS
SUPPORT PEOPLE,
ETC.

FIGURE 2

57

aimed at the improvement of the status of the elderly, added new complexities to an already complicated and pressure-filled life pattern. Observers in various professional fields have stated that the demands of our present society exceed the coping capacity of most individuals to help themselves in stress-related situations and create new challenges to the service professions (Golant and McCaslin, 1979; Meyer, 1976).

The point I am trying to make here is that between people's ability to cope on their own and their dependence on social and health services, a "buffer-zone" could be created by the kind of information services that would empower people to cope more effectively, and would assist service providers in both meeting and, whenever possible, preventing acute needs for service. Practitioners and researchers in various professions and disciplines, must begin to work together led by the recognition that both *problem solving* by individuals and *problem counseling* by various professionals depend on high quality information and data. In order to consider the potential impact of alternative approaches to a problem or situation, the decision of both consumers and service providers should be preceded by gaining access to existing knowledge. This is a demanding principle that is too often ignored because of lack of time and information awareness.

Trends that result in new public policy and service needs have been extensively charted in the literature of social gerontology. I would like to turn our attention to these well-known social phenomena from the perspective of the new information needs they created for consumers and service providers. The following points should be considered as examples rather than elements in a comprehensive review.

*Changes in the Social Domain*

Increasing numbers of older persons in the population

Differentiation between the young-old and the old-old

More demands for health and social services as well as for preventive measures

*Changes in the Information and Knowledge Domain*

Diversification of information needs and problems of assessment (rural elderly, minorities handicapped, etc.)

Changing assumptions of how people seek and use information

New kinds of information products resulting from the diversification of work

*Changes in the Social Domain (Cont.)*

Increasing economic pressures and problems of people on fixed income

The need for adequate measurements for economic status, poverty threshold, health status and environmental influences

The need for scientific, socioeconomic and legal intelligence in the planning, management and evaluation of services

Citizen participation and the need for information and data to support advocacy efforts

The rise of cultural considerations in recognizing the needs of various groups in society and people in developing countries

Changes in social stereotypes and resulting shifts in the knowledge base

Increasing need for interdisciplinary work in research and program development and resulting communication needs

Recognition of life-span crises and stress situations and the role of support networks

Reliance on technology and ethical, philosophical and legal problems thus created

*Changes in the Information and Knowledge Domain (Cont.)*

Fragmentation and scattering of problem-focused information in the literatures of various disciplines and professions

Keener data orientation; the need for social, health, environmental, quality of life and poverty indicators

Increased demands for scientific, medical, legal and other specialized information by nonspecialists

Concern with the utilization of knowledge for policy, practice and personal coping

Need for baseline data and recognition of the influence of social stereotypes

Proliferation of large-scale information systems and problems of access at the community level

The increased need for communication between researchers and practitioners

Availability of information technologies and the problem of assessing their use for various groups, individuals and situations

| *Changes in the Social Domain (Cont.)* | *Changes in the Information and Knowledge Domain (Cont.)* |
|---|---|
| More leisure time and decreasing economic means for leisure activities and mobility | Need for direct access to information systems by people as well as the need for intermediaries who synthesize, translate and repackage knowledge |
| | Need to understand the economics of information and measures of productivity and effectiveness |

The above examples simply aim at generating dialogues between researchers and practitioners who are concerned with understanding the role improved information delivery might play in the lives of elderly people and the work of gerontologists. There are questions that need to be explored and practices that must be tested and evaluated. The elderly are not only partners in this exploration, but they are the most valid source of knowledge and experience. This recognition is a link between practitioners and researchers upon which many other forms of cooperation can be built.

Parallels between *human service delivery* and *information delivery* have often been observed. Both depend on rigorous need assessment and a combination of ethical, legal and psychological considerations. Both activities are difficult to evaluate because of the inadequacy of current measurement techniques. Efforts of testing have concentrated mainly on the approaches and tasks used in human services and information services, rather than on the change, if any, they brought about in the recipients or in their lives. As larger and larger numbers of people are becoming dependent on the service system, policy experts have suggested that services should be considered public utilities. Similar recommendations have been made for the creation of information utilities to assure a more equitable access to information upon which individual choices can be made. The direction in both fields is toward an integrated "package" for the user in preference to piecemeal referrals to separate services and information resources, respectively. The quality of information services is as difficult to define as that of health, mental health and social programs. Beattie (1976) characterized one of the major principles of social services in words that accurately described the main motivation of information services as well: "A guiding philosophy of services to the aging is to assure that their provision supports the individualized and unique needs and capacity of older persons" (p. 620).

While these parallel trends in the human service and information professions can facilitate the identification of areas where joint efforts for knowledge utilization could be undertaken, they can also spawn occasional misconceptions. One of the most striking examples is the wide-spread belief, evidenced in the literature, that "Information and Referral" (I&R) is the only productive interface between human and information services. In comparison, until recently very little attention has been given to internal decision support and management information systems (Bowers and Bowers, 1977). Even more neglected are the potential benefits of information services that would utilize external bibliographic and numeric data bases and large-scale information and data systems in order to provide support to human service personnel. The way I&R services, management information systems and information support services could be linked to enhance each other's functions has generally not been recognized.

Two complimentary models, a centralized information support system and a decentralized information sharing network, have been developed and tested by field research at the Syracuse University School of Information Studies.

## *A Centralized Model: The Gerontological Information Program (GRIP)*

The prototype program was developed and tested between 1976 and 1979 as an information dissemination mechanism to create closer links between academic gerontologists and practitioners who work directly with the elderly. The program used a three-pronged approach, integrating (1) an information dissemination and support system, (2) research on information needs and uses, and (3) individualized training of graduate students of various disciplines in the utilization of information and data resources.*

Established jointly with the All-University Gerontology Center under Administration of Aging funding, GRIP conducted an assessment of the information needs of 65 administrators and service providers in four types of organizations: geriatric centers/nursing homes; senior citizens' groups and centers; specific services; and umbrella or coordinating agencies. A structured questionnaire was used in person-to-person interviews. Analysis of the data concentrated on problems that the respondents needed information about (funding sources, transportation, nutrition, the isolation of older people, etc.); types and sources of information they used; and the kinds of information

---

*For information about GRIP II, contact the All-University Gerontology Center, Syracuse University, Brockway Hall, Syracuse, NY 13210 (315) 423-2790.

support they would prefer (Figure 3). We found that current methods of accessing information were not successful for this population as indicated by the lack of solutions to problems or dissatisfaction with the solutions (Brindle, Dosa and Gee, 1977).

Based on the need assessment study, GRIP has developed two kinds of services for human service personnel working with the aged: A newsletter on new information sources and modes of obtaining them, and an information support system answering queries. Examples of topics included legislation, small-area demographic data, minority elderly needs, architectural barrier problems, etc. When necessary, information was extracted from the

## OBJECTIVES OF GRIP

### NEED ASSESSMENT AND EVALUATION

THE TWO STUDIES INTENDED TO MEASURE:

**PRE-SERVICE NEED ASSESSMENT 1977**

TYPES OF PROBLEMS SERVICE PROVIDERS NEEDED INFORMATION ON

WAYS OF INFORMATION ACQUISITION

SOURCES OF INFORMATION

PREFERRED FORMS OF INFORMATION SOURCE

TYPES OF INFORMATION

EXTENT TO WHICH THE INFORMATION OBTAINED WAS USEFUL

**RETROSPECTIVE EVALUATION OF THE SERVICE 1979**

ACTUAL USE OF THE INFORMATION OBTAINED FROM GRIP

   O KINDS OF ACTIVITY THE INFORMATION WAS USED FOR

   O TYPES OF BENEFITS (ASSISTANCE, SOLUTIONS, CONTACTS, ETC.)

INFORMATION SHARING BEHAVIOR

USER-PERCEIVED QUALITY OF INFORMATION

USER-PERCEIVED VALUE OF THE INFORMATION SERVICE

FIGURE 3

sources and organized for the user; for instance, alternative state programs to aid the elderly with rising energy costs were reviewed and summarized for a policy maker. The results of all searches are evaluated, edited, and packaged in the form, length, depth, and detail most appropriate for the requestor. As a by-product of the system, GRIP has computerized its own data base containing sources relevant to the planning, management and evaluation of community services to the elderly. The utilization of information is difficult to evaluate because of the interpretations by different people of what is useful and what is not useful information.

The evaluation was aimed at three user groups: community-based users in Onondaga County, community-based users elsewhere; and academic users at both Syracuse University and elsewhere. Preliminary findings about the reactions of the two groups of service providers to the information dissemination service were reported to the meeting of the Gerontological Society (Dosa and Brindle, 1979). These findings should be considered as exploratory only.

During a nine-month period forty-three people who worked with the elderly in Onondaga County used the GRIP information service. Thirty-four could be reached and asked for formal feedback by means of a self-administered questionnaire. Thirty-three responded—a rate of 97%. In addition, questionnaires were sent to forty-three GRIP users located elsewhere. This group included individuals from the national and international gerontological community. Thirty-two responded, a return rate of 77%. The respondents were asked to indicate the kind of activity for which they used the information received from GRIP; what kinds of ''benefits'' did the information provided by the GRIP service lead to; and how did the information service generally help them in their job-related roles or why was it important to them.

It was in the area of information sharing that GRIP proved to be especially useful to the human service agencies and practitioners. The information packages prepared by GRIP for the requestors were not only used but passed on to co-workers and administrators. In both Onondaga County and elsewhere most of the GRIP users shared the information with someone else. They usually shared with co-workers in their own agency (66.7% of the local respondents, and 53.1% of the users elsewhere). This led us to believe that the information dissemination service stimulated internal communication in the recipient agencies.

Occasionally the information was shared with administrators (21% of users locally, 12.5% of users elsewhere) and with colleagues outside of the recipient agencies (18% locally and 15.6% elsewhere). This means that the number of users of information provided by GRIP reached an audience far larger than the original user group.

In reference to some of our original questions concerning the potential role of an information dissemination and support service to human service practitioners we found that:

> Service providers don't have ready access to information and the kind of query answering service GRIP has offered.

> The GRIP prototype provided a connecting link between information and referral services, management information systems and other information services by supplementing rather than duplicating their function.

> This kind of information dissemination service can make an impact if there is a gerontologically sensitive and trained staff of intermediaries to (a) search national and international information resources, (b) utilize computer technology in the interest of human needs, (c) individualize the packaging of information in response to queries, and (d) through community contacts, anticipate as well as formally measure needs.

> The joint training of graduate students form various disciplines builds good researcher-practitioner relations and prepares individuals for a new role in society: the gerontological information disseminator.

> The prototype information service, thoroughly documented, could be utilized by state offices of aging, area agencies on aging, academic gerontology centers and gerontological associations by using the proto type GRIP methods and processes.

> Services to the elderly could be enhanced by greatly needed information support to service providers and older persons' organizations.

This investigation opened up a number of new research questions. What would be the optimum way of packaging the content of information retrieved by computerized and manual searches? How can "value" be conceptualized? Could measurements be developed and standardized to assess the value of information to users? What happens in "chains" of information delivery as results are passed from one user to another? How can "failures" of support be measured by ascertaining problems that were not solved by the information and reasons for the lack of success? What are ways of cost recovery for an information support system?

*A Decentralized Model: The Health Information Sharing Project (HISP)*

Under sponsorship by the National Library of Medicine, this four year field research is examining a new mode of improving the flow of health-related information and data in a community. The main objectives are: (1)

experimental development of a prototype decentralized information sharing mechanism, and (2) empirical evaluation of HISP in terms of benefits to the participating organizations as well as its potential problems. HISP (a) identified unpublished health related studies, surveys, data collection efforts, policy analyses, training packages and other sources produced by local agencies that were presumed to be available through informal communication, (b) determined the location, forms and terms of access, (c) made this information available to health agencies and organizations in the form of a computerized resource directory, (d) facilitated information exchange by the development of a network of agency contact persons or gatekeepers, (e) interfaced with information and referral (I&R) services, management information systems and libraries (Figure 4).

We used a field experiment to (a) examine exchange patterns of participating agencies and information use, (b) obtain data on the effect of HISP in enhancing interagency contacts and (c) show whether an information sharing arrangement such as HISP has promise. During the first year, we carried out face-to-face interviews with 284 staff members at health agencies in Syracuse, N.Y.

In the second year, a post-measure was administered to establish to what extent, if any, the introduction of the HISP resource directory and network of gatekeepers contributed to quantitative and qualitative changes in the agencies' information sharing patterns. Staff at forty-five very diverse agencies formed a pool of respondents: directors, administrative personnel, specialized health professionals and medical/health science librarians. Returns were received from 216 persons. The evaluation was generally favorable. Recommendations in reference to the contribution of the project were broken down as follows:

| | |
|---|---|
| Discontinue | 17.3% |
| Continue with major modifications | 9.4% |
| Continue with minor modifications | 29.1% |
| Continue as is | 44.1% |

Gatekeepers were quite active not only within their agencies but also externally, forming links between health workers from other agencies and personnel from their own institutions. We found that the role of the gatekeeper was crucial in diffusing the availability of HISP throughout the agency. Methods of diffusion were identified. All those using the resource directory (two thirds of the sample) said that HISP helped their information seeking. three major factors attributed to positive attitudes toward HISP:

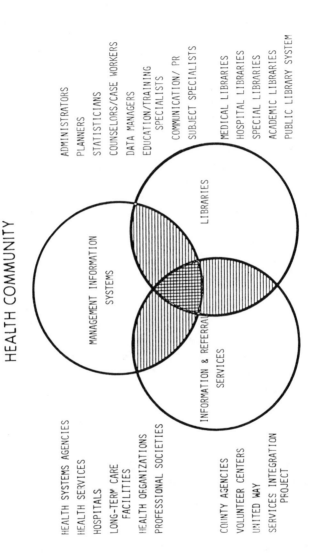

HEALTH COMMUNITY

FIGURE 4

66

—satisfaction with the overview of available resources,
—reliance on people in information seeking,
—information accessed through HISP helped to avoid duplication of work,
(Dosa, Genova and McGill, 1978).

The Syracuse prototype has been replicated at two new sites within Region II of the Regional Medical Library Network: Binghamton, N.Y. and Albany, N.Y. The aim is to study the effects of the HISP network in three settings characterized by different social, economic and organizational structures. In the three communities, a total of 145 organizations are participating in HISP. The inventory of locally produced unpublished information resources has been completed at the two new sites and the resource directories are being distributed. A combined list of gatekeepers in all three communities has been distributed to initiate interaction among the three sites. On December 13, 1979, an awareness raising workshop in Syracuse brought together 70 health professionals and librarians to discuss ways of updating the resource directory and identifying information related problems. A questionnaire collected data on the areas of specialization (aging, alcoholism, cancer, child abuse, nutrition, etc.) of the participants.

A field experiment is evaluating the effects of HISP at the two new sites. Responses to the pre-measure questionnaire are currently being collected. In addition to this investigation, HISP developed thorough project documentation and constructed an information base by the review of the cross-disciplinary literature of networking.

New problems identified by this process are: What type of agency should take responsibility for the ongoing updating of the HISP resources and gatekeeper lists? Can a decentralized network maintain itself or does it need a focal initiative and management? Can the network be utilized for purposes other than interagency information sharing? Can it be successfully merged with an information support service to participants? These questions, together with the GRIP research described above, led us to a new research agenda.

## Research Utilization Synergy

During our field research, we became keenly aware of the value of practitioner-researcher communication. Without feedback from colleagues and suggestions for specific problems that merit further exploration we could not have overcome certain conceptual barriers. This experience led us to focus on information dissemination and utilization in both our literature review and our own practices.

The ongoing transfer of research findings to practitioners and policy makers should be seen as an integral part of rendering knowledge socially useful. In addition, program-related experience is accumulating in the form of feasibility studies, program analyses and evaluation reports: a fugitive kind of literature. Legislative, regulatory and judicial information is becoming inseparable from effective program management. These resources are needed at certain times by decision makers, but they cannot easily be tapped because of their vastness.

The theoretical and review literature on knowledge and information utilization has burgeoned in recent years (Geer, 1977; Human Interaction Research Institute, 1976; Zaltman and Duncan, 1977). Two general models might be distinguished: (a) utilization of directed research performed specifically for end users and goals (the problem-solving model), and (b) the ongoing monitoring and tapping of generalizable research findings for users (the enlightment model) that "provides the intellectual background of concepts, orientations and empirical generalizations that inform the professional activities of the user" (Weiss, 1977, p. 544).

Knowledge utilization is most often seen as a one-way process from the vantage point of either the research or the decision maker. The influence of individual attitudes and interactions can hardly be overestimated, especially in interdisciplinary fields. Several recent investigations might be cited as relevant to this symposium. Most of them are empirical studies of organizational behavior, the diffusion and adoption of innovation and the use of communication channels in service organizations (Gerstenfeld, 1978; Nuehring, 1978; Wigand, 1976). Greer (1977) provided an analysis of diffusion studies concerning health care organizations published since 1960. Theories fell into three broad groups: adoption of innovation by individuals; organizational attributes influencing the adoption process; and decision making in health institutions.

The traditional view of the process of knowledge utilization encompasses three phases: the dissemination of research findings, utilization by persons in the field of practice and application to the solving of practical problems. We suggest several changes in the traditional model:

- A careful differentiation between the concepts of knowledge utilization and information utilization. In the literature, "knowledge" is usually understood as the outcome of theoretical or empirical investigation. In this sense, "knowledge utilization" is restricted to the use of research findings only. "Information utilization", on the other hand, can be interpreted as the use of any source that helps in problem solving, decision making or updating one's view of the world. Information utilization by the health professional may include program descriptions, financial analyses, federal and state regulations or economic reports.

- As part of the utilization process, the *acceptance* of information on the part of the user plays a major role and needs to be studied.

- Feedback from practitioners, especially the identification of problems that were not helped by the information, is as important in the process as the dissemination phase.

The role of intermediaries such as "information counselors" needs more exploration. As shown in Figure 5, in the interaction between researchers, intermediaries (counselors) and practitioners the flow of information must be a two-way process. Intermediaries act as facilitators and information switchers and should never come between the researcher and the practitioner except in building direct links between them.

"Information counseling" has been defined as the interactive process by which an information practitioner (1) assesses the information needs of an individual or organizations, (2) determines the optimal ways to fill such needs and assist the client in information use, and (3) assures systematic follow-up and feedback in order to evaluate the effectiveness of counseling (Dosa, 1977).

Assistance in information utilization may be provided at four levels: (a) bibliographic reference to an information source, (b) document delivery, (c) the content of information based on the analysis of the information source(s) and (d) evaluated and interpreted information for advocacy. Information counselors can optimize their effectiveness by accessing, on behalf of their client, not only formal information systems but also human resource networks.

The model of information counseling emanates from concepts embedded in the literature of three areas. It is a composite and expansion of three previous models: information and referral; adult educational counseling; and the library reference interview. Each of these previous models has been confined to applications in a particular professional context: social work, adult education and library/information service. The new approach incorporates interdisciplinary features and thus it is applicable to the information needs of various people, environments and problem areas.

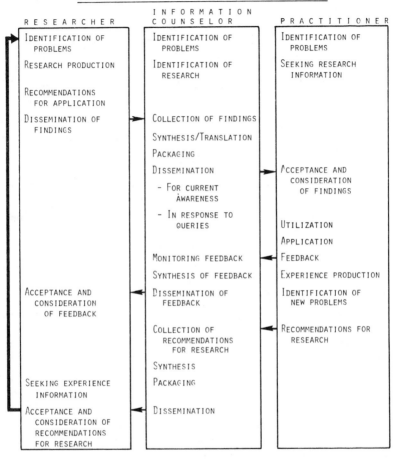

FIGURE 5

*In the Philosopher's Words*

In sharing with you our attempts to find ways to improve information utilization in social service and health care agencies, I hope that a discussion has been started that will continue long after this symposium adjourns. I will say thanks for the privilege of being here today by quoting the philosopher Michel Philibert:

In gerontology and in geriatrics, the progress is not from knowledge to know-how and thence to know-how-to-be, but only the other way around, from a quality of being to intervention and through intervention to knowledge (Philibert, 1979, p. 391).

## REFERENCES

Beattie, W.M. "Aging and the social services" in Binstock, R.H. and Ethel Shanas, eds. *Handbook of aging and the social sciences*, New York, N.Y., Van Nostrand Reinhold, 1977.

Bowers, G.E. and N.R. Bowers. *Cultivating client information systems*. Rockville, MD. U.S. Dept. of Health, Education and Welfare, Project SHARE, 1977 (Human services monograph series 5).

Brindle, E.A., M.L. Dosa and G.M. Gee. "A Prototype gerontological information program" paper presented at the 30th Annual Scientific Meeting of the Gerontological Society, San Francisco, November 21, 1977. *Proceedings*, White Plains, N.Y. Knowledge Industry Publications, Inc., 1977. p. 7.

Caplow, Theodore. *Toward social hope*. New York, N.Y. Basic Books, 1975.

Dosa, M.L. *Information counseling*, in *Information*, Science Associates/International, Inc., vol. 7, No. 3, 1978.

Dosa, M.L. and E.A. Brindle. "Impact of information and data support for practitioners working with the elderly" paper presented at the 32nd Annual Scientific Meeting of the Gerontological Society, Washington, D.C., November 29, 1979 in *Gerontological Information Systems and Services*, Syracuse, N.Y., School of Information Studies, 1980 (Research Study no. 5).

Dosa, M.L., B.L. Genova, M.J. McGill. *Development and evaluation of health information sharing: Executive summary*, 1977–78, Syracuse, N.Y., 1978.

Geer, A.L. "Advances in the study of diffusion of innovation in health care organizations" *Milbank Memorial Fund Quarterly*, 55 (Fall 1977) pp. 505–532.

Gerstenfeld, Arthur. "Innovation and health care management" *Hospital and health services administration*, (Spring 1978) pp. 38–50.

Golant, S.M. and Rosemary McCaslin. "A Functional Classification of services for older people", *Journal of gerontological social work*, 1:3 (Spring 1979) pp. 187–209.

Holland, T.P. "Information and decision making in human services" *Administration in mental health*. (Fall 1976) pp. 26–35.

Human Interaction Research Institute. *Putting knowledge to use: A distillation of the literature regarding knowledge transfer and change*, Los Angeles, CA, 1976.

Meyer, C.H. *Social work practice: The changing landscape*. New York, N.Y., The Free Press, 1976.

Nuehring, E.M. "The character of interorganizational task environments" *Administration society*, 9:4 (February 1978) pp. 425–447.

Philibert, Michel. "Philosophical approach to gerontology" in Hendricks, Jon and C.D. Hendricks, *Dimensions of aging: Readings*. New York, Cambridge, Mass., Winthrop Publishers, 1979, pp. 379–394.

U.S. Congress. House, Committee on House Administration. Policy Group on Information and Computers. *Information policy: Public laws from the 95th Congress*, Washington, D.C. Government Printing Ofice, 1979 (96th Congress, 1st Session, Committee print).

U.S. General Accounting Office. *Conditions of older people: National information system needed*, Washington, D.C. 1979 (HRD-79-95).

U.S. National Commission on Libraries and Information Science. *National information policy*, Washington, D.C. Government Printing Office, 1976.

U.S. Office of Technology Assessment. *Selected topics in federal health statistics*, Washington, D.C. Government Printing Office, 1979.

Vinson, E.A. and D.L. Chewning. *The National Rural Information Clearinghouse of the National Rural Center*, Interim report 1976–1977, Final report 1977–1978. Washington, D.C. Department of Commerce, 1978. (ERIC document ED 178 038).

Weiss, C.H. "Research for policy's sake: The enlightment function of social research" *Policy analysis*, 3 (1977) pp. 531–545.

Wigand, R.T. "Communication and interorganizational relationships among complex organizations in social service settings" paper presented at the International Communication Association, Portland, Ore., 1976.

Zaltman, Gerald and R. Duncan. *Strategies for planned change*, New York, N.Y., Wiley, 1977.

# THE NATIONAL ARCHIVE OF
# COMPUTER-READABLE DATA ON AGING

Susan B. Haberkorn
Michael W. Traugott

The development of data archives containing computer-readable resources relevant to the study of aging reflects the growing awareness that a variety of social scientific and medical models can be appropriately applied to solving problems in this area and that greater advantage must be taken of substantial investments already made in underutilized original data collections. Relatively immediate research returns and policy analyses are possible from the extended analysis of such resources conducted in response to pressing national needs. And such efforts can be achieved without the lag and expense associated with launching new studies each time a new question is raised about problems of the aged or the process of aging. At the same time, the use of increasingly complex research designs associated with ever larger data bases is straining the computational resources available to the average researcher, in both technical and financial terms. With computer-readable data files becoming available in larger numbers, the challenge is for archives to develop means for simplifying access to increasingly obstreperous datasets on a routine basis and for training a new cohort of secondary analysts in their use.

The National Archive of Computerized Data on Aging (NACDA) is a joint project of the Inter-university Consortium for Political and Social Research (ICPSR) and the Institute of Gerontology (IoG) at The University of Michigan. It is sponsored by the Administration on Aging (AoA) and the National Institute on Aging (NIA) to provide a mechanism to make selected data on aging accessible to a wide range of users both in academic institutions and the aging network.

The availability of computer-readable resources through a social science data archive serves both a scientific and an administrative function based upon the concept of secondary or extended analysis. The underlying notion of secondary analysis is that no principal investigator ever exhausts the full analytic potential of a dataset. In one sense, this is simply the case because any single researcher, or group of researchers, has a particular, and in this sense limited perspective on the data associated with a model based upon a specific set of operationalizations. As the process of theory development and testing occurs, or, more likely in the case of progress in the social sciences, as additional disciplinary perspectives are brought to bear in the field, data collected for one purpose come to be viewed quite differently in conceptual and operational terms by other researchers.

From a scientific perspective, the significance of archival data rests upon the principle of replication, the notion that confidence in the validity of a relationship between two or more variables is increased by the number of times and variety of settings in which it can be reproduced. As an elemental fact, the original relationship should be reproducible by secondary analysts in the original data base. But more importantly, data archives provide a central repository for multiple collections of data in which the same relationship may be tested in a variety of research contexts.

From an administrative point of view, archival resources represent a cost-effective means of increasing research opportunities and, implicitly, results. And these cost reductions are available in time as well as money. The greatest single cost involved in the conduct of research is usually for data collection and processing. These cost reductions are associated primarily with the complexity of the research design and the number of units of analysis or observations required. But beyond the initial data collection effort, considerable resources must be devoted to transcribing information to computer-readable form and then checking the resulting data matrix for consistency and other technical errors. Then inevitable problems which are found must be resolved and corrected before analysis begins. In addition to financial resources required for research and support staff, field costs, and the like, this process often requires substantial periods of time, even years in the case of extensive longitudinal studies. The alternative, when appropriate archival resources are available, is construction of a research design based upon existing data, followed by a search through documentation for meaningful operationalizations of important theoretical concepts. The documentation must be of sufficient quality to enable a researcher who did not participate in the original data collection effort to understand the project designs and goals, the field work, and the analytic methodology. And this is one of the most important archival functions.

Although there is often an iterative process by which the secondary analyst must modify an original design in accord with available data resources, this process consumes relatively little time. When the selection of archival data has finally been made, copies of the files can usually be delivered to the analyst in a matter of days or weeks at a cost effectively equal to the cost to duplicating a magnetic tape. If archival resources are sufficiently rich and diverse, then, they provide an unusual and effective opportunity for meaningful research by skillful analysts and policymakers. And this research effort can be carried out for the marginal costs of staff and computer costs, implying that a fixed amount of available research dollars will support more analysis on more research questions. A wide variety of important datasets relevant to the study of aging are currently available from a number of sources.

In this context, the National Archive of Computerized Data on Aging has been organized around three major program elements: the acquisition and processing of computer-readable data, the provision of training in the use of these resources, and services to facilitate access and utilization of the data. NACDA provides a mechanism which allows and encourages researchers, agency personnel, and others concerned with aging to bring empirical data and advanced analytical tools efficiently and effectively to bear in research, policy and program development, and evaluation. The consequences will be improved knowledge, enhanced capacity to apply that knowledge to practical needs and to the solution of concrete problems, and improved ability to develop and implement effective policies and programs.

Now in its fifth year of operation, the program draws upon the resources, facilities and personnel of ICPSR and the IoG, as well as those of The University of Michigan in general. The Consortium, with an institutional membership of over 240 colleges and universities, serves social scientists around the world by providing a central repository and dissemination service for machine-readable social science data; training facilities in basic and advanced techniques of quantitative social analysis; and resources for facilitating the use by social scientists of advanced computer technology. The IoG, in keeping with its legislative mandate has developed programs with a three-fold approach including instructional programs to increase the quantity and quality of manpower for research, teaching and service provision in the field of gerontology; research to find solutions to specific problems of the later years and to contribute to social policy; and service components to support and strengthen the capabilities of public and voluntary agencies to serve the aged more effectively. Through these programs the IoG has developed a worldwide network of relationships with professionals in the field of aging.

While knowledge and technical skills of the NACDA staff are substantial, the development of a truly representative national resource requires that they be augmented. The conceptual framework for the archive depicted in

Figure 1, explicitly incorporates three separate groups to assist the staff in the identifiction and acquisition of the most significant datasets, in aging-related fields, the establishment of training priorities for researchers and practitioners, and the optimization of access to the data.

A *National Advisory Committee* is composed of distinguished scholars who are active in the field of aging, drawn from the social sciences, the humanities and the biomedical sciences. Also serving on this committee are aging network representatives from the National Association of State Units on Aging (NASUA) and the National Association of Area Agencies on Aging (N4A).

Through the involvement of this committee, the program receives advice on acquisitions and the establishment of archival priorities both from the informed consultation of active researchers and from the knowledge provided by professional practitioners in the field of aging. The committee meets annually and aids in the determination of priorities for data acquisition and processing, advises in the design and staffing of training activities, and in the development and expansion of modes of access and utilization of program resources.

A *Research Panel* composed of outstanding scholars at The University of Michigan has been established to provide additional expertise. These individuals are readily available for meetings on a regular and more frequent basis, and to consult with the project staff as questions arise that are associated with their particular areas of expertise. The Research Panel is of singular value in identifyng data resources for acquisition, in leading to contacts with researchers at educational institutions and government agencies, and as a source of assistance in encouraging researchers to provide the archive with data that they have collected. The members of The University of Michigan Research Panel are also expected to provide a link with other resources at The University of Michigan with which the project staff may not be familiar. Finally, guidance is received from these individuals in developing NACDA training programs.

An *Agency Liaison Group* has also been created which consists of staff members of the Administration on Aging and of the National Institute on Aging. They meet quarterly with the four senior staff of NACDA to assist in identification of datasets important to their respective agencies and to present to this group an identified set of lacunae in existing data, indicating areas where the agencies might consider directing research support to fill in the gaps. The Agency Liaison Group members also play a key role in disseminating information about the archive to their constituencies through their various communication networks.

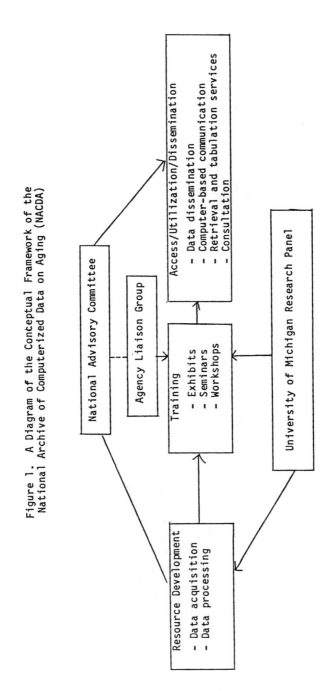

Figure 1. A Diagram of the Conceptual Framework of the National Archive of Computerized Data on Aging (NACDA)

*Purpose*

The central purpose of NACDA is to optimize the effective and efficient use of empirical data for the purposes of research and of policy and program formation and assessment in the field of aging. The project also contributes to improvement of the standards of data collection and analytical methodology in the field of aging, to more systematic data collection efforts, and to reduction of redundant and wasteful investments in such efforts. At the same time, the project also makes the potential benefits of the very large investments of government and private agencies in collection of empirical data more fully realizable.

Drawing upon such resources as sample surveys, the United States Census, biomedical and health services data, and administrative and case records, the utility of empirical data for applied and basic research into social processes is wisely and generally recognized. Empirical data combined with the analytical tools of statistics, mathematics and computational machinery have provided a basis for greatly improved knowledge and understanding of social phenomena. As yet, however, the study of aging and the aged, particularly in relation to broader social processes and institutions and to biomedical factors, has not profited from these resources to the same degree as numerous other fields of social inquiry. The reasons for this situation are many. Chief among them are the relative lack of effective access on the part of researchers involved in the study of aging to advanced tools of analytical inquiry, and the coincidental lack of access to needed empirical data resources. The latter consideration has also worked to slow movement of researchers from other fields to the study of aging.

Despite their value for extended applications, data collected by individual researchers and research groups are frequently not available to others or are made available only after a substantial and debilitating time period has elapsed. Even when made available, moreover, the form of such data collections often frustrates use. Documentation that adequately describes study design, sampling characteristics, reponse rates and data collection procedures is often lacking; extensive data ''cleaning'' is frequently required to correct errors and eliminate idiosyncracies; and the technical form often requires extended reprocessing and reformating. Thus effective use by other researchers is prevented, and the benefits of the original investments in data collection are not realized.

Data produced by the government frequently present difficulties as well. The direct cost of acquiring these data is often high. In many cases ''over purchasing'' is necessary; more data must be acquired, at higher costs, than are required for a specific application. Data from government sources are required for a specific application. Data from government sources are usually not supplied in readily-usable technical form; and after acquisition, the costly and time-consuming tasks of reprocessing, subsetting and reformating must still be faced. The consequence is often that use of these data is precluded by all but the few well funded or highly determined researchers located at institutions with advanced and well developed technical facilities. Thus, the ability of researchers to employ these data and, indeed, even the direction of research applications are determined in considerable degree by the accidents of institutional location.

The consequences of these difficulties are even more severe for applications of data to program and policy development, administration and evaluation. The greater immediacy of these tasks means that extended delays for reprocessing, reformating and subsetting usually cannot be tolerated, and, in any event, the facilities required to carry out this work are usually unavailable.

The potential value of empirical data and advanced analytical methods and tools for the development, monitoring and evaluation of public policies and programs is not yet widely recognized. Nevertheless, in the area of aging, as in other areas of public concern and responsibility these resources afford means to (a) more reliably identify and anticipate problem areas and groups, (b) design and estimate the direct and indirect effects of policies and programs, (c) monitor the efficacy and equity of their implementation and administration, and (d) evaluate their impact, effectiveness and utility. Enhanced use of such resources could lead not only to substantially improved policies and programs, but also to avoidance of adverse and unanticipated policy consequences. As a case in point, empirical analysis of available data relating to the structure of benefits for the aged and to present and prospective population characteristics would have revealed and prevented the adverse impact of the recent modest increase in Social Security payments upon the Medicaid entitlements of many older Americans.

Through NACDA, the Inter-university Consortium for Political and Social Research and the Institute of Gerontology administer a major program which directly addresses and substantially reduces these interrelated problems. Briefly NACDA contains: (1) National surveys (e.g., the Harris poll of myths and realities on aging); and (2) Government-related studies (e.g., selected census data, and the National Center for Health Statistics' survey of nursing homes and other health care facilities, and the Social Security Administration's retirement history and longitudinal survey of beneficiaries). A detailed description of the NACDA holdings can be obtained by writing to NACDA, Box 1248, Ann Arbor, MI 48106.

*Provision of Data*

Data from NACDA are accessible to users via three modes: (a) entire datasets on magnetic tape which can be manipulated and analyzed at an individual's resident computing facility; (b) in customized formats, either as subsets of cases and/or variables on magnetic tape or as tabulations generated according to specifications; and (c) direct access to data on The University of Michigan computing facilities through a national computer network.

Direct dissemination of data collections and custom subsets of collections on *magnetic tape* is the preferred means of access to archived data by researchers in the academic sector.* Agency practitioners and administrators, however, lacking computational facilities may find other data access options more practical and satisfactory.

One option, likely to be most desirable to the majority of the aging network personnel, is the provision of *custom data services*. Under this approach, users request specific custom displays and/or retrieval of data. For example, project staff can retrieve a specific data element associated with the requestor's geographic area of responsibility. Requests for custom data services are refined in consultation with project staff until definition of content, the data to be used, their format, and the data reduction and analysis procedures to be employed are explicit. The program then delivers the custom output suited to specified needs and purposes. To date, most such requests are simple and straightforward. However, this approach readily allows the extension of custom services employing advanced analytical procedures to meet the more complex needs and interests of agency personnel.

On a less formal scale, selected printed information such as distributions and cross-tabulations of data can be distributed to planners upon request. Recent experiences of the archive staff in responding to requests for assistance suggest a number of ways in which the available data sets can be utilized by area agencies on aging and other governmental agencies charged with planning and coordination on behalf of older people. Since most of the data in the archive come from large national samples, the user has considerable latitude in expanding analysis of these data beyond their original objectives. Many analyses can be performed that were not considered as part of the original research design, particularly those that compare younger and

---

*Information about the availability of NACDA resources on magnetic tape can be obtained by writing to Ms. Janet Vavra, Technical Director, ICPSR, Box 1248, Ann Arbor, MI 48106.

older respondents. The archived data are also valuable for conducting preliminary investigation of phenomena to determine which are worth more detailed research.

The second option to magnetic tapes, is *direct data access*. Practitioners, administrators and researchers without adequate local computational equipment can directly access the facilities of The University of Michigan. The Michigan Terminal System (MTS) is a terminal oriented, time-sharing operating system which allows employment of the full range of typical analytical capabilities. Given access to a computer terminal, MTS is available through Telenet, a national computer network. The direct access approach allows immediate access to program data and analytical capabilities irrespective of geographic location or the limitations of local facilities. It allows users to inexpensively employ a sophisticated computational system, extensive and complex data resources, and the full range of statistical and analytical capabilities. Technical assistance is provided by ICPSR to instruct individuals in the use of the system and to aid in the solution of any problems encountered. It has been found that with only minimal instruction, individuals are able to make effective use of these resources in a highly independent fashion. The special seminars and the short courses described later in this paper provide introduction and encouragement to remote use of MTS.

The data services enumerated above serve a wide range of individual and organizational needs. They provide access to empirical data and analytical resources for individuals at varying levels of technical competence. These approaches meet the needs of individuals with access to advanced technical equipment, but also eliminate obstacles to the use of data and analytical resources for those without local access to that equipment.

## Consultation and Technical Assistance

To promote and support the dissemination and use of project data, consultation and technical services are provided to individuals who are interested in the use of the NACDA data and the computing facilities at The University of Michigan. One important element of assistance in this area is the ability to provide a researcher with information about the possibility for alternative designs or measures which might be used to address a particular problem, indication of whether or not appropriate data are available, and the most efficient data access mode to employ.

Technical consultation services are provided to assist users with limited technical experience who seek to employ archival data resources. Guidance is provided on the characteristics and use of the major social science software systems currently available and their suitability for applications. For those who may choose to use The University of Michigan facilities, consultation is also available specifically on the operation of the OSIRIS system and other available analytical software alternatives, including SPSS and MIDAS (the Michigan Interactive Data Analysis System).

Technical consultation is also provided to individuals who have local computing facilities. it is necessary to know particular characteristics of a local computer installation and to apply this information in developing appropriate specifications for generating copies of datasets. This service is important in order to guarantee that each requestor, having located relevant data resources, receives them in a technically usable form, compatible with local computing facilities.

*Training Programs*

Training programs are offered both by the ICPSR and the IoG in conjunction with their summer training programs.

The seminar offered by the ICPSR provides the context for application of a variety of quantitative skills to a range of policy-related issues associated with aging and the aged.\* The purpose of the seminar is to stimulate research interest in the area and to provide training and aid in the development of the skills of individuals presently working in this field. The instruction is provided by senior social scientists with quantitative research expertise and experience and includes "on hands" experience in computer analysis of archival data collections.

In addition to the ICPSR seminar, special short courses are also offered during the summer by the IoG.\*\* These courses are designed with the particular needs of agency personnel, administrators and planners in mind and provide practical training and experience with computers and computer-readable data bases. Information on all courses can be requested in writing from the NACDA staff.

*Conclusion*

NACDA provides alternative means of access to empirical data, analytical resources and powerful computational facilities to serve the diverse needs of multiple clienteles. The program utilizes and extends the resources of two

---

\*For information on these offerings write to Henry Heitowit, Coordinator of Training Program, ICPSR, Box 1248, Ann Arbor, MI 48106.

\*\*For information on these offerings write to Larry Coppard, Director of Education, 520 E. Liberty St., Ann Arbor, MI 48109.

major organizations—the IoG and ICPSR. It capitalizes on the extensive facilities of The University of Michigan and extends the utility of resources already created through support provided by the Administration on Aging and the National Institute on Aging. Through the program, users of widely varying technical and methodological sophistication can rapidly and effectively employ advanced capabilities and resources for policy, program and research purposes.

# INFORMATION/DOCUMENTATION ON AGING IN AN INTERNATIONAL CONTEXT: AN ANALYSIS BY AN INFORMATION USER

George Thomas Beall

Although there are differences in the political, economic, and cultural circumstances among the USA and other industrialized nations of the world, the many similarities of their circumstances makes useful a continuing consideration of how such foreign countries deal with their aging populations. Especially useful as bases of comparison are those Western European nations which became "old" in the last quarter of the 19th Century, according to United Nations' criteria which describe a country as "old" when its aged represent 7% or more of its total population. In the industrialized nations of Western Europe, the presence of an "old" population prompted the development of approaches to and experience with meeting the needs of older people well before the USA was confronted with similar requirements. As a consequence, knowledge of their historic experiences, as well as their current practices in dealing with an aging population holds the potential to provide instruction for us in the USA.

Yet, as this report is designed to substantiate, we (the professional community in aging with the USA) do not consistently and systematically draw upon the experiences of other nations in our information gathering and utilization habits. Nor have we established comprehensive means by which we and other nations can keep abreast of one another's literature and documentation. In developing formal information systems and services, we, and the European nations for that matter, tend to stop short of considering the systematic treatment of materials published outside of our national or

Mr. Beall is currently, Associate Director, Housing Technical Assistance Program, ICSG, 425 13th Street, N.W., Suite 840, Washington, D.C. 20004.

Much of the work reported upon in this article was undertaken as part of the International Information/Documentation Study in Aging, of which the author was Principal Investigator. This study, in part supported by the U.S. Administration on Aging, was conducted for the International Center for Social Gerontology (ICSG). Among the general purposes of the ICSG is to advance the social welfare of older people through the dissemination of information on an international basis.

*85*

language boundaries. This situation exists in spite of the widespread acceptance among gerontologists of the legitimacy of the concept of a "world gerontology" (Kaplan, 1975; Shock, 1975).

In the report which follows, symptoms of this limited pattern of cross-national information transfer in the field are identified, and, from the perspective of an information user, causes are analyzed. In view of the fact that a principal cause is suggested to be the national or linguistic myopia which characterizes the formal information transfer chain in the field, recommendations are offered on how formal systems for information exchange might expand and otherwise improve their treatment of foreign-source and foreign-language materials.

### Current Practices in the Use of Foreign-Source and Foreign-Language Documentation

Information-gathering and utilization patterns observed within the gerontological community, especially in its social and behavioral components, appear to build upon foreign-source and foreign-language documentation to a very limited degree. This conclusion was drawn from an analysis of contents of major articles published in the two major American journals in the field, *The Gerontologist* and the *Journal of Gerontology* (hereafter cited as *Journal*). The review of articles in the *Gerontologist* was over a 10-year period from 1966–1976; that of the *Journal*, the more scientific and research-oriented of the two publications, was for a one-year period, 1976.[1]

The initial conclusion drawn from this analysis was that the authors publishing in these two journals during the study periods revealed a high level of interest in topics related to international or foreign developments in aging. Over one-third of the articles in *The Gerontologist* and over four-fifths of those in the *Journal* were found to reflect some degree of interest in such activities, either in thematic content or in citations to foreign references.

However, in spite of this evidence of interest in foreign activities, analysis of the references cited in the articles revealed a low rate-of-utilization (at least a low rate-of-citation) of foreign-source and foreign-language documentation. Only slightly more than 10% of the total references cited in *The Gerontologist* were citations to materials which treated cross-national concerns in aging, and many of these citations were to American materials which

---

[1] The details of this analysis are reported in Beall, George Thomas and Mulak, Susan. "perspectives on the Availability and Utilization of Foreign-Source Informational Materials in Gerontology."

treated foreign or international activities as a major focus. While articles in the *Journal* revealed an overall higher rate of reference to foreign-source materials, this rate was due primarily to the very high frequency of reference to such materials among the *Journal's* medical and biological manuscripts. Among social and behavioral manuscripts published in both journals, reference to the utilization of foreign-source or foreign-language materials was infrequent.

When foreign references were cited, they tended to be citations to books and periodicals originally published in the English language, in predominantly English-speaking countries. This pattern is evidenced in both the book and journal sources which were repeatedly cited as references. Whereas most references on foreign or international activities in the field were cited only once, each of eleven books originally published in English, were cited in at least seven articles. One such reference source, *Old People in Three Industrial Societies* (authored by E. Shanas and associates, published by Atherton Press, New York, 1968) was cited in 35 articles. Other repeatedly-referenced book sources consisted of:

Beyer, G.H., & Nierstrasz, F.H.J. *Housing the Aged in Western Countries*. Elsevier, Amsterdam, 1967.

urgess, E.W., (Ed.) *Aging in Western Societies*. University of Chicago Press, Chicago, 1960.

.lark, M., & Anderson, B.G. *Culture and Aging: An Anthropological Study of Older Americans*. Charles C. Thomas, Springfield, 1967.

Hausen, P.G. (Ed.) *Age with a Future*. Munksgaard, Copenhagen, 1964.

Havighurst, R.J., Munnichs, J.A., Neugarten, B.L., & Thomae, H. *Adjustment to Retirement*. Van Gorcum, Assen, 1969.

Simmons, L.W., *The Role of the Aged in Primitive Societies*, Yale University Press, New Haven, 1945.

Townsend, P., *The Family Life of Old People*. Routledge & Kegan Paul, London, 1957.

Townsend, P., *The Last Refuge*. Routledge & Kegan Paul, London, 1962.

Tunstall, J., *Old and Alone*. Routledge & Kegan Paul, London, 1967.

Welford, A.T., *Aging and Human Skill*. Oxford University Press, London, 1968.

While a total of 160 distinct journal sources were cited as sources of information on foreign activities at least once during the study periods, the journals most frequently referenced were, as noted, English language. The most repeatedly cited journal sources included: *Lancet* (England); *The*

*Gerontologist* (USA); *Human Development* (Switzerland); *Occupational Psychology* (England); *British Medical Journal; Nature Ergonomics* (England); *Gerontologia Clinica* (Switzerland); *Journal of Gerontology* (USA); *Medical Journal of Australia; British Journal of Psychiatry; International Journal of Social Psychiatry* (Canada); *Canadian Psychiatric Association Journal*; and *Canadian Medical Association Journal.*

This heavy rate of dependence on reference materials originally published in English decreased somewhat in the *Journal* manuscripts. While over 70% of the references to foreign activities in *The Gerontologist* were to such materials; this percentage dropped to slightly less than 50% among the manuscripts in the *Journal.* Journal sources published in Japan, the Netherlands, and the Scandinavian countries, while infrequently cited, were cited more frequently in the *Journal* than in *The Gerontologist.* This citation of foreign-language sources, however, tended to be more frequent among biological and medical manuscripts and on topics that resisted strict national or cultural identity.

When source material on aspects of aging across nations was cited, there was a consistently higher rate of utilization of references published seven or more years before their date of citation. This dependence upon "older" informational materials characterized references in the *Journal* to as great a degree as was evidenced in *The Gerontologist.* In the *Journal* survey, 57% of all foreign references utilized were published five or more years before their date of citation; slightly more than 41% were published seven or more years before citation. This compares to rates of 55.2% and 43.4% respectively for such references cited in *The Gerontologist.* It is interesting to note that dependence upon "older" source materials increased over the 10-year survey period of *The Gerontologist.* Of note is the fact that concurrent with this increase in the "age" of a reference source was an increase in the utilization of reference materials from France and from other countries in which English is not the predominant language. There was also an increase in the citation rate of book sources as references, as opposed to journal articles and other types of informational materials. Hence, the presence of increased translation requirements, as well as a differential rate of use of materials based on their length and potential complexity, might account for increases in the time between date of publication and date of citation.

## Explaining the Trends Noted in the Use of Foreign Documentation

The obvious conclusion to be drawn is that published articles in gerontology, outside of its biological and medical components, tend to reflect a common pattern of usage of foreign-source and foreign-language materials, regardless of whether in a research journal or one more practice oriented. This pattern is characterized by a relatively strong indication of interest in foreign activities, which is coupled with a low rate of utilization of foreign-documentary sources. Where foreign documentation is cited, such sources tend to be "older" materials, originally published in English, principally in English-speaking countries, some five or more years before the date of citation. Consequently, with the USA gerontological community not having evidenced a high degree of utilization of current foreign materials, it is not surprising that in the development of new, national, automated channels for the collection, organization, and transmission of informational materials in the field, foreign documentation is given little attention. For example, the SCAN (Service Center for Aging Information) being developed by the U.S. Administration of Aging, as a matter of policy, tends to exclude foreign-source and foreign-language materials. The questions to be addressed now are why is the situation what it is, and what can be done to improve it.

## Growing Volume of Informational Materials

Could it be that the volume of foreign documentation potentially available for reference is itself small? Have other nations, especially those in Western Europe, not witnessed a continuing and comparable growth and professionalization in the aging field, with a condomitant increase in the informational materials being produced therein? Available evidence suggests that the answer to each of these questions is no.

In fact, knowledge of current developments abroad reveals that ours is not the only country in which evolutionary forces in the development of the field have generated a tremendous increase in the volume of information being produced, transmitted, and consumed. Growth of the knowledge base in the field, as reflected in its printed representations, has necessitated movement away from small, specialized collections of materials and from dependence upon finding gerontological knowledge scattered throughout the various traditional disciplines. The growth in the volume of and demand for literature in the field has pushed various nations, the USA included, toward the application of advanced documentation practices. To wit, the increasing need to provide bibliographic order and access to the growing body of documentation on aging, has prompted such developments in the addition to the U.S. SCAN system, as: (a) national cooperation in the creation of an aging thesaurus and faceted classification scheme in Great Britain, among Age Concern and the National Corporation for the Care of Old People, two prominent aging organizations; the Corporation also maintains a national register of research in aging; (b) in France, a computerized aging information storage and retrieval system was established within the Centre Internationale de Gerontologie Sociale; while it is believed that the automated system is not operating currently, there are known to be formal, collaborative information exchange projects among the major French national organizations with interests in aging; (c) the initiation of a West German information and documentation center within the Deutsches Zentrum fur Altersfragen (Berlin), which serves as a national center for literature and research documentation, as well as a statistical data bank; and (d) the development of a computerized system for the organization and retrieval of information on research in aging with the Dutch Gerontolisch Centrum (Nijmegen), where interest has also been expressed in the creation of a national center of information and documentation.

At the international level, best evidence of the felt-need to respond to this proliferation of information and informational materials in the field is to be found at the United Nations. There, within the Social Development Division, and information exchange system in aging has been established. That system, while not primarily concerned with the acquisition and distribution of non U.N.-produced publications, serves as a point of access and referral to information resources at international and national levels, and has been developed with a view toward establishing a world-wide network of professional correspondents in the field. The U.N. information system produces a periodic *Bulletin on Aging*, which includes an annotated bibliography.

## Relevant Materials Not Easily Accessed

A paradox exists in that despite such evidence that internationally, the volume of informational materials in aging is proliferating, the USA professional community appears to draw lightly upon this international well-of-knowledge and documentation. In fact, our review suggests that utilization rates of foreign documentation have fallen. Two potential factors present themselves as explanations for this phenomenon, namely the: (1) qualitative characteristics of the materials available, and (2) inaccessibility of much of the documentation being produced and which is, or could be of potential relevance to the interests of the American professional community.

Although the scope of this examination has not included an assessment of the qualitiative characteristics of the non-USA literature being produced or utilized, it had been built upon the assumption that similarities in the circumstances of aging, as well as parallel developments in the growth and professionalization of the field, make for points of comparability among nations. Support for this position derives from books and authors cited early on and is underscored in reports emanating from the Columbia University cross-national studies of social services. Although giving recognition to differences of emphasis and program, the Columbia reports, for example, amply document the comparability of structures and approaches between the USA and other European nations in responding to the social needs of their older citizens (Kahn & Kamerman, 1975; Kamerman, 1976). Assuming that the growing volume of literature addresses these structures and approaches, among other topics, there is indeed a basis for concluding that the international literature, even if it were to be qualitatively inconsistent, is of general relevance to an American audience.

Having concluded that there is a growing volume of foreign literature of potential relevance to American authors, it is proposed that such materials are not more widely utilized because of factors related to their accessibility. In fact, the survey evidence suggests that in their utilization of foreign materials on aging, American authors have operated in congruence with a tenet of information science which holds that information will tend not to be used whenever it is more painful and troublesome for a person to have information than not to have it (Mooers, 1960). As has been observed, foreign reference sources have tended to be older materials originally published in English. Both such characteristics combine to increase user access, thereby making older, English-language materials the least painful or troublesome to utilize.

If securing knowledge of their availability is the first step in accessing foreign documents, then increased accessibility (as well as the more incremental growth of knowledge characteristic of the hard sciences) also begins to explain why biological and medical manuscripts tend to reflect more widespread use of foreign documentation. The fact is that historically, the major bibliographic tools of access to foreign literature on aging have emphasized biological and health-related contents. The SHOCK Bibliography,[2] for example, typically provides wide coverage of foreign publications; however, it has traditionally excelled in treatment of materials in the medical and biological disciplines. And, the *Excerpta Medica* volume on gerontology and geriatrics, although it contains abstracts of social science literature, emphasizes treatment of medical materials.

A dilemma arises, however, when it is acknowledged that even when a reference is available and accessible, the information and data contained within it may often not be easily interpreted or assimilated by most poten-

---

[2] The SHOCK Bibliography is a guide to current publications in gerontology and geriatrics published regularly in the *Journal of Gerontology*.

tial users. Even when a source is secured, it frequently presents translation requirements which introduce overwhelming impediments to assessing and assimilating the knowledge which it contains. Such requirements include not only translation from one language to another, but also translation from one cultural context to another, as well as between disciplines. As a result, when the means of securing knowledge of foreign activities in the field has meant pursuit of available documentation, with the concomitant requirements to identify, obtain, translate, and assimilate such materials, the difficulties encountered in the process are judged to have frequently operated against their use.

*Improving Access to and Promoting Utilization of Foreign Knowledge*

In the absence of evidence of easy access to and substantial utilization of a broad-based, international body of literature and documentation in the field, especially in its social and behavioral components, what are the means by which the American professional community keep abreast of foreign developments? The absence of comprehensive systems for the collection, organization, and exchange of information among nations cannot be interpreted to mean that the task of cross-national information exchange has been ignored. Rather it reveals the dependence which has been placed on a relatively few seminal documents and on periodic, narrowly-focussed, and typically non-systematic forms of information exchange. Drawing upon the journal analysis previously reported, as well as other findings from the ICSG international documentation study, it is concluded that the information transfer chain in the field of aging primarily has been dependent upon:

- periodic international conferences;
- reports of foreign activities which appear from time to time in American journals and periodicals, and, to a lesser extent, episodic utilization of foreign journals, primarily English-language;
- landmark books, few in number, published by American and foreign authors, primarily in English;
- discrete, one-time, cross-national research projects;
- such tools-of-access to the world's literature in the field which exist; principally, on a regularly basis, *Excerpta* Medica and the SHOCK Bibliography in the *Journal of Gerontology*;
- episodic interests of such organizations as the United Nations, the World Health Organization, the Organization for Economic Cooperation and Development, the Council of Europe, the International

Federation on Housing and Planning, and a host of other professional and political agencies and organizations which have aging among a wide-range of multi-national interests;

• the information products and services of such international aging groups as the International Association of Gerontology, the International Federation of Aging, and the International Center for Social Gerontology, all of which have international information exchange as an organizational objective, but none of which serves as a comprehensive source of access to the world's literature in the field; and

• informal networks of colleagues and professional contacts who constitute an "invisible college" or personalized system of information exchange by letter, telephone, or visit.

While all such means have contributed substantially to the transfer and application of knowledge of other nation's activities in aging, not one serves as a continuous, systematic, and comprehensive source of access to information and data between and among nations. Hence, the limitations present in information management in aging internationally, parallel those which other investigators (Miller and Cutler, 1976), have found nationally. While all existing approaches contribute to the field, no one existing approach adequately serves the overall field.

For those committed to improving the formal systems by which information is collected, organized, and made available to potential users, international aging or a "world gerontology" presents itself as an area in which improvements in the formal information transfer chain can be proposed. And, given the increasing significance of the world's "aging" population, it can be argued that improvements should be undertaken, as they hold the potential to contribute to the scope, depth, and quality of national aging policies and research; to spark innovation; and to otherwise promote the development of the field. Improvements in the means by which "national lessons in aging" are communicated, also hold the potential to facilitate planning in those countries which have yet to face the aging of their populations.

*Improving the Organization of and Access to International Documentation*

In proposing improvements in the formal information systems in aging across national boundaries, emphasis must be placed on recognition of the ultimate desirability of a comprehensive source responsible for the collection, organization, and retrieval of the multi-national and multi-disciplinary literature in the field. The scope and cost of such an enterprise, however, coupled with the difficulties to be faced in having such a source serve the multifaceted information needs of the wide community of information users, makes the establishment of a single center unfeasible and inappropriate.

An achievable recommendation for improving the organization of and access to documentation, however, is that of calling for international cooperation designed to provide, at a minimum, comprehensive, coordinated bibliographic order to materials extant and being produced in aging. This cooperation would be primarily among the emerging national centers of information and data, specialized collections maintained by national and international organizations and research centers, and other national and international organizations in aging and aging-related disciplines. What is proposed as desirable is an integrated international network of such information centers and collections, and not a large-scale, monolithic, and unresponsive new structure.

The cooperation and coordination called for might take several forms, including (1) national coordination, under the aegis of the developing national centers of information and data, and through which information/documentation systems and services and other types of information resources operating generally within a national sphere, would be coordinated; (2) language area coordination in which a single information/documentation center might collect and make available the literature from a common language region of the world; and (3) coordination of information/documentation activities among information sources and research centers operating in specialized topical areas, such as housing; health care; or adult education.

Experiences in other fields (e.g., Medlars/Medline and the International Nuclear Science System) appear to have demonstrated the feasibility of such international coordination in order to provide bibliographic order and access to the world's literature in their areas of interest. The applications of computerized information processing techniques increase the feasibility of coordination and the ease with which it can be undertaken, both in the information/documentation collection and storage stages, as well as in the production and exchange of various information services and products.

The best time to plan for international, cooperative activities of the type proposed here, would certainly be early in the development of the national, language, or specialized topical area centers, before the press of competing national or organizational demands substantially reduces the resources available for investment in an international exchange effort. The evidence indicated that this has not been done. For example, the SCAN system of the U.S. Administration on Aging, now several years into its development, does not even provide for the solicitation of and entrance into its files of materials produced outside the U.S. This type of cultural or linguistic myopia will certainly operate against the ease with which a formal international network might be initiated. However, the ultimate objective to be achieved seems sufficiently meritorious that it is proposed that such obstacles be confronted and, hopefully, overcome. In fact, the developing national centers of information in aging are actively encouraged to initiate or strengthen dialogue among themselves. And, it is proposed that representatives of these developing national centers might be constituted as an international information retrieval system in the field. This coordinating body might initiate planning for this system through consideration of such issues as: the subject interests and types of information and data to be included in an international exchange; the classification schemes to be utilized; the standards for the mechanics of information transfer, including the problem of translating from one language to another; the targets and procedures for the production of desirable information products and services; and the roles and responsibilities of various participating centers. It would be appropriate for an appropriate international organization, for example, the United Nations or the International Association of Gerontology, to take the leadership in convening such a group.

*Promoting the Utilization of Foreign Documentation in the U.S.*

As suggested in the current patterns of usage of foreign informational materials by U.S professionals in aging, however, awareness of and access to foreign materials does not mean that such materials are or can be utilized, especially by persons in the social and behavioral areas of the field. For this reason, it is also proposed that consideration should be given to the establishment of one or more information analysis centers whose functions would be to compile, digest, and "package" foreign information in forms which would make it most useful to American audiences. The hallmark capacity of such an information analysis center would be its analytical and evaluative capacities, maintained among a staff of international subject experts. This capacity would differentiate it from a specialized library, or a document depository, or an information service of the abstract-bibliography variety, although in fact the proposed center(s) might perform each of these functions to a degree.

Among its primary products and services, such a center could provide English translations of primary-source materials and prepare critical reviews, monographs, or equivalent publications on the state-of-the-art in selected aspects of aging internationally. An information analysis center might also develop models of exemplary programs, techniques, and approaches, and otherwise promote the utilization and application of knowledge of foreign experiences in the field. Through its activities, the center would seek to build upon and sustain the valuable momentum of interest in foreign activities which, under current conditions, seems to be generated now from time-to-time by discrete cross national studies and from occasionally published reports.

Three distinct audiences hold the potential to be served by the center(s). They include:

1. researchers, teachers, planners, students, and others who would be expected to have need for specific information of a detailed and technical nature. For them, a useful product of such a center might be a technical monograph on a specific topic.
2. practitioners and direct service providers who would be expected to desire comparative, less scientific, less detailed, and more easily assimilated information. Useful products to serve this audience might include reports of model approaches and programs in aging, or a newsletter.
3. older adults and the general public, who might hold generalized interests in aging and who would benefit from knowledge presented in popular, easy-to-read formats.

It is acknowledged that the tasks of securing, distilling, and applying "foreign" knowledge can be complex. If one assumes, however, that progress is rooted in knowledge, then it appears inexplicable that we have failed to more actively pursue and build upon all sources of knowledge available to us, and that we have not been more consistently guided in our pursuit of this objective in the establishment of systems and services to organize and disseminate information in our field. It seems clear that we can and should do better.

## REFERENCES

Beall, George Thomas. *Findings and Conclusions: The International Documentation Study on Housing and Related Facilities and Services for Older Adults.* International Center for Social Gerontology, Washington, D.C., 1975.

Beall, George Thomas and Mulak, Susan. "Perspectives on the Availability and Utilization of Foreign-Source Informational Materials in Gerontology." *Gerontologist*, 1977, 17, 537-544.

*The Gerontologist*, March, 1966 - June, 1976, Vol. 6, No. 1 - Vol. 16, No. 3.

*Journal of Gerontology*, 1976, Vol. 31, No. 106.

Kahn, A.J., & Kamerman, S.B. *Nor For The Poor Alone: European Social Services*. Temple Univ. Press, Philadelphia, 1975.

Kamerman, S.B. *"Community Services For The Aged, The View From Eight Countries."* *Gerontologist*, 1976, 16, 529-37.

Kaplan, J. Editorial. *"The Interfluence of World Gerontology: The Moral Application."* *Gerontologist*, 1975, 15, 194.

Miller, E.H., & Cutler, N.E. "Toward A Comprehensive Information System In Gerontology: A Survey of Problems, Resources, And Potential Solutions."*Gerontologist*, 1976, 16, 198-205.

Mooers, C.N. Editorial. "Mooers Law On Why Some Retrieval Systems Are Used And Others Are Not." *American Documentation,*1960,11,3.

Shock, N.W. Ediorial. "Why an International Association of Gerontology?" *Gerontologist*, 1975,15,195.

# SELECTIONS OF MULTIDISCIPLINARY
# INFORMATION SOURCES

Janet R. Bailin
Sherry Morgan

What is old? This question is asked again and again by people of all age groups. Philosophers have pondered it for centuries; scientists have been searching for answers; policy makers and service providers attempt to develop definitions and measurements for it; and artists have been portraying it in innumerable ways. Now the scientific study of social gerontology is building an extensive body of accumulating knowledge around this complex question. Jon and C. Davis Hendricks introduced their collection of readings in *Dimensions of Aging* (Winthrop Publishers, 1979) in these words: "To respond to the question 'What is old?' gerontologists draw on studies and insights from the biological sciences, social sciences, and the humanities. None of these alone is sufficient to describe or understand the process of aging. While human aging has many parallels with the way other biological organisms age, only humans can analyze the process of their own aging. Accordingly, gerontology—the study of the entire aging process—is a multifaceted specialty drawing from traditional bodies of literature while building its own" (p. 1).

As the population of older persons increases in modern societies both in numbers and in percentage of the total population, so does our interest in the findings and practices of social gerontology. The field deals with the behavior and social role of the aging individual, society's response to the growing numbers of the old, and the demographic and cultural aspects of the aging of entire societies. With the expansion of government involvement, research programs, advocacy organizations and institutions, also the production of information has accelerated. The proliferation of primary sources and the bibliographic apparatus—indexing and abstracting services, data bases, directories, research inventories—to access them, present a formidable challenge. Embedded in practically every discipline and professional area,

Janet R. Bailin is Information Specialist, Interamerica Research Corporation, Washington, D.C., and Sherry Morgan is Medical Librarian, Hartford Hospital, Hartford, CT. This paper was written when the authors were at the School of Information Studies, Syracuse University, Syracuse, NY.

information resources relevant to aging include institutions, collections and personal expertise. The richness and diversity of these resources would preclude any attempt on our part to identify and reference a representative range of them even by type or category.

The objective of this essay is modest. We simply intend to highlight a few examples of those organizations and information sources that span several specialties. The criteria for selection included (a) the consensus of positive reviews in the literature or (b) the unusual nature of the information accessed by the source (e.g., statistical data on aging, teaching aids, research in progress). The focus is on gerontology in the United States, because world-wide developments and their literature would merit a publication of much larger scope than ours.

We were not guided by the intent to offer a recommended selection for a gerontology collection. Rather, we asked the question of what kinds of works would give librarians and the managers of special collections a starting point in getting acquainted with the multi-disciplinary information needs of social gerontology and what sources would help them to find updating information in the future. For more in-depth bibliographic information and references in various subjects (education, health, retirement, etc.), the reader is referred to the excellent keys to the literature listed in the section " Toward Bibliographic Access" in this essay. Clearly, this is not a "guide" to gerontological information sources in the conventional sense. Still, we hope that it will provide some hints that will inspire the user to penetrate more deeply into the field.

## *Historical Perspectives*

It is not unusual for relatively new multidisciplinary fields to look to the past to identify social and behavioral phenomena that might explain the emergence of concerns that merged into the new field of study. Without the historical and philosophical dimension, it might be harder for members of various disciplines to understand each other's approaches.

Joseph T. Freeman's *Aging: Its History and Literature* (Human Sciences Press, 1979) is a beautiful small book. Its major part is devoted to various bibliographies of ancient and contemporary works on geriatrics and gerontology. The first chapter is a survey of the history of gerontology and geriatrics throughout the world exploring the relationships between approaches to aging in different periods and cultures. *Roots of Modern Gerontology and Geriatrics* edited by Gerald Gruman (Arno Press, 1979), presents writings by Frederic Zeman, Gerald Gruman and Joseph T. Freeman, among others. The papers by Frederic Zeman, written between 1942 and 1950, describe the work of key people who prepared the way for modern gerontologists. J.T. Freeman not only established one of the first geriatric clinics in the United States, but also pioneered the history of gerontology in this country by his paper published in 1938. *Old Age in the New Land: The American Experience since 1790* by W. Andrew Achenbaum (Johns Hopkins University Press, 1978), is a landmark treatment of the changes in the perception of the elderly in American society. The important transition between 1865 and 1914, when specialization and European influences became apparent in the negative way the aging process was viewed, is treated with great sensitivity.

*In Search of the New Old: Redefining Old Age in America, 1945-1970* by Richard B. Calhoun (Elsevier-North Holland, 1978), discusses the philosophical development of social gerontology in the United States, the different theories of the role of the elderly in society, and various approaches to the process of aging. The author also traces the development of social programs and political reforms in the United States. For those interested in a quick overview of social gerontology prior to the twentieth century and through the 1930s, James E. Birren and Vivian Clayton's paper ''History of Gerontology'' may be the answer. Included in *Aging: Scientific Perspectives and Social Issues* (Van Nostrand Reinhold, 1975), it traces the development of the study of aging beginning with the attitudes of the ancients toward the old as reflected in their myths.

The emergence of gerontological works in various disciplines and professions may be studied by either turning to the historical treatises of biology, psychology, social work, sociology, and other fields themselves and culling references to age-related investigations and practice, or searching out historical chapters in comprehensive reviews of gerontology. In the first category, there is Elaine M. Brody's short overview of social work practice with the elderly, ''Aging'' in the *Encyclopedia of Social Work* (National Association of Social Workers, 1971, pp. 49-95). In the same context, we found insights on the foundations of early gerontology in *Main Trends of Research in the Social and Human Sciences (UNESCO, v. 1, 1979).* The second approach can be illustrated by Peter Laslett's ''Societal Development and Aging'' in the *Handbook of Aging and the Social Sciences* (Van Nostrand Reinhold, 1977, pp. 87–116) and Klaus F. Riegel's ''History of Psychological Gerontology'' in the *Handbook of the Psychology of Aging* (Van Nostrand Reinhold, 1977. pp. 70–102).

78/95

Searchers for trends, events and pioneers marking the beginnings of multidisciplinary work in aging will find that the early issues of journals usually contain glimpses into the past. Frank Lawrence's paper, "Gerontology" in the *Journal of Gerontology*, (1:1, 1946, pp. 1-11) presents an historical perspective as seen in the 1940s.

## *Conceptual Landmarks and Aids: Handbooks and Texts*

As research activities expanded in the mid-twentieth century and theory-building in the various disciplines investigating the aging phenomenon progressed, the need to synthesize these theories and concepts into a body of knowledge that was uniquely gerontological, was recognized. This effort of integration resulted in the publication of a series of handbooks. Handbooks organize accumulated knowledge into systematic structures, and document the process by an analysis of the most significant literature. Textbooks bring together in a more condensed form the established fundamental theories and developments in a field as aids to teaching.

Most handbooks in gerontology have been published within the past two decades. However, pioneering works identifying past accomplishments and emerging research needs had been produced much earlier, for example Vladimir Korenchevsky's "The Problems of Aging and the Ways and Means of Achieving the Rapid Progress of Gerontological Research," in *The Social and Biological Challenge of Our Aging Population* (Columbia University Press, 1950). The most significant definitive compilations (not all in social gerontology), appeared as the well-known "trio" of the University of Chicago Press: *Handbook of Aging and the Individual—Psychological and Biological Aspects*, edited by J.E. Birren (1959), *Handbook of Social Gerontology—Societal Aspects of Aging*, under Clark Tibbit's editorship (1960), and E.W. Burgess' *Aging in Western Societies—A Survey of Social Gerontology* (1960). Even though not strictly a handbook, the latter contains fundamental information that rounds out the coverage of the other two.

A set of three new handbooks in the late 1970s synthesized knowledge that had accumulated in a decade. *The Handbook of Aging and the Social Sciences*, edited by R.H. Binstock and Ethel Shanas (Van Nostrand Reinhold, 1976), traced the theories of aging through several disciplines and professional areas. For instance, the relationship of aging to economics, law and housing was documented. Many of the contributing authors related historical background to current research; therefore, publications cited should be used in the context of their period. J.E. Birren and K.W. Schaie prepared the *Handbook of the Psychology of Aging* (Van Nostrand Reinhold, 1977), covering four sections: "Background," "Biological Basis of Aging and Behavior," "Environmental and Health Influences on Aging," and "Behavior and Behavioral Processes." Although not in social gerontology, but still an integral part of the new "trio," the *Handbook of the Biology of Aging* (Van Nostrand Reinhold, 1977), edited by Caleb Finch and Leonard Hayflick, reviews the "status of the basic biological knowledge of gerontology." Two chapters are especially interdisciplinary in approach: "The Evolution of Aging and Longevity," and "System Integration," the latter by Nathan W. Shock.

In recent years, many other fine compilations have appeared, for example, *Social Forces in Later Life* by R.C. Atchley (Wadsworth Publishing Co., 3rd edition, 1980), an excellent introduction to social gerontology. Biological and psychological aspects of aging are reviewed, as well as special situations related to late life. Responses of society to the elderly are considered: social relationships, economy, governmental concerns and politics. James E. Birren and R. Bruce Sloane's *Handbook of Mental Health and Aging* (Prentice-Hall, 1980), is an important addition to the field. Contributions from national and international experts cover the social, psychological, and physiological aspects of the mental health of the elderly. *Contemporary Social Gerontology: Significant Developments in the Field of Aging* by B.D. Bell (Thomas, 1976), is a collection of works by sixty authors dealing with demography and ecology, health, economics, housing, minority elderly, and retirement. More specialized is Sylvia Sherwood's *Long-term Care: A Handbook for Planners, Providers and Researchers* (Spectrum of Hallstead, 1975), which is mentioned here as an example of a work addressed to several audiences in gerontology.

*Aging and Society* is a three-volume edited by Matilda White Riley, et al. (Russell Sage Foundation). Volume 1: *An Inventory of Research Findings* (1968), volume 2: *Aging and the Professions* (1969), and volume 3: *The Sociology of Age Stratification* (1972), deal with the results of social gerontological research, the practical implications of the findings, and their contributions to sociological theory, respectively.

Many fine textbooks will have to be omitted from this essay because of space limitations. The following example will demonstrate the utility of a truly multidisciplinary approach that attempts to define and delineate geriatrics and gerontology in relation to each other. *The Textbook of Geriatric Medicine and Gerontology*, written by J.C. Brocklehurst (Churchill Livingston, 1978), covers section on "Gerontology," "Geriatric Medicine," and "Medical and Community Care." Very well received by reviewers, the text is now in its second edition.

## Introduction to Policies and Services

One of the central concerns in social gerontology which needs the attention of professionals from various backgrounds, is the formulation of policies that create or change service programs. For an international background on aging populations and service development today, one might begin with *Socio-Economic Policies for the Elderly* (Organization for Economic Cooperation and Development, 1979), published in Paris. This slim book charts some universal trends and interrelationships such as demographical changes, work, and retirement. Policies and programs for health, education, and pensions in France, Germany, Norway, and the United States are discussed. In addition to an overview of recent developments in labor force participation and the future of retirement income systems, the publication examines programs and activities designed to enhance the social participation of the elderly. The chapter on the United States is also available as a separate publication of the U.S. Department of Labor and is entitled *Socio-Economic Policies and Programs for the Elderly*. Erdman Palmore is the editor of a fine new contribution to the literature of social trends: *International Handbook on Aging: Contemporary Developments and Research* (Greenwood, 1980).

As we turn to the social scene in the United States, we find that an excellent background for policy considerations has been charted by *Changing Landscape: Social, Economic and Political Trends in America and their Implications for Older Americans*, edited by C.S. Harris and R.C. Blank (National Council on the Aging, 1980). *Future Directions for Aging Policy: A Human Service Model* is a report of the Subcommittee on Human Services of the House Select Committee on Aging (1980). The Federal Council on the Aging's *Policy Issues Concering the Minority Elderly* (Department of Health and Human Services, 1979), presents an overview of four populations: Black Americans, Pacific Islanders/Asian Americans, Hispanics, and American Indians. The study delineates several issues to be addressed in Federal policy-making for the minority elderly and makes recommendations for the future.

Douglas and Monica Holmes gave us a useful source on major service programs for the elderly. The *Handbook of Human Services for Older Persons* (Human Sciences Press, 1979), was designed to inform gerontologists about Federal, state and local agencies, relevant legislation, and services. Suggestions as to the implementation of the services are also offered. One of the chapters focuses on the significance of Information and Referral (I & R) services to older persons. *The Aging Network: Programs and Services* by

Donald E. Gelfand and Jody K. Olsen includes description of programs set up in individual communities throughout the United States which attempts to meet the needs of the elderly in a variety of ways. In the same framework, *Counseling the Elderly: For Professional Helpers who Work with the Aged*, edited by G.L. Landreth and R.C. Berg (Thomas, 1980), represents services by the direct relationship of counselor and client.

Carroll L. Estes' *The Aging Enterprise* (Jossey-Bass, 1979), is a critical evaluation of service programs and relevant policies. Estes analyzes the impact of Federal, state, and local agencies, legislation, and programs on the elderly, and assesses the successes and failures of public policy. While presenting a rather negative picture of the problems of policy implementation, she also investigates the roots of problems and changes needed to initiate improvements. One of the reliable and effective sources where one can look for policy-related information is the *National Journal Issue Book*. Written by experts including Bernice L. Neugarten and Robert H. Binstock, one of the "issue books" (1980), examined major policy concerns in aging for the 1980s.

## Toward Bibliographic Access

Bibliographies probably form the most heterogeneous group in the family of reference works. There is no dearth of these prolific access providers in social gerontology. There are numerous bibliographies available on specific topics such as health care of the elderly, nutrition or retirement, as well as general sources that include all aspects of aging. It is only difficult to find up-to-date listings that can keep up with the fast-moving changes in primary publications.

The classic—now retrospective—source is Nathan W. Shock's "Current Publication in Gerontology and Geriatrics" that has appeared from 1962 to November 1980 in each issue of the *Journal of Gerontology*, with annual cumulative author indexes in the September/November issues. This series was preceded by *A Classified Bibliography of Gerontology and Geriatrics* (Stanford University Press, 1951), with supplements in 1957 and 1963. Listings included journal articles, conference proceedings, monographs, research reports, and many other publications in this country and abroad in a wide range of subjects. The "Shock bibliography" will be greatly missed. An evaluation of this major tool was carried out by Margaret B. Monroe in her paper: "Analysis of the Shock Bibliography in Providing Bibliographic Access in Gerontology," presented at the Gerontological Society's 30th annual scientific meeting in 1977 (ERIC document no. 171 252).

In respect to retrospective bibliographic searches, the extensive references in the six basic handbooks discussed earlier may be used as starting points. Although uneven in coverage and quality, these references comprise a bibliographic framework for the fundamentals of gerontology. Further citations will be found in the following four reference works that collectively provide a broadly based coverage.

*Selected Bibliographies* by Lilly Ho (New York State Office for the Aging, 1977), is still representative of the diversity of gerontological topics, although it is becoming rapidly outdated. *A Guide to Reference Sources in Gerontology* by Barbara Perkins (Scripps Foundation Gerontology Center, 1977), offers a good basis one can use for updating. Willie M. Edwards from the Institute of Gerontology, University of Michigan, and Frances Flynn from the Center for Community Health and Medical Care, Harvard University, joined their expertise in compiling *Gerontology: A Core List of Significant Works* (University of Michigan, 2nd ed., 1981). References are classified by subject and indexed by author and title. *Gerontology: An Annotated Bibliography* by M. Leigh Rooke and C. Ray Wingrove (University Press of America, 1977), carries concise and to-the-point annotations.

We will make no attempt to include here bibliographies on special aspects of social gerontology except as examples. Areas of research and practice where information is in great demand may be illustrated by "citizen participation in policy making," "death and dying," "the economics of aging" and "minority aging." These are complex multidisciplinary fields of study where new publications are dispersed in the literature of several disciplines and professions. Relevant organizations might provide a good starting point. For example, the National Center on the Black Aged published the *Topical Annotated Bibliography on the Black Elderly* (1979). Many multidisciplinary topics are covered by the Vance Bibliographies, although mostly without annotations. "Citizen Participation in Urban and Regional Planning" (1977) and "Planning for the Aging" (1979) are examples of compilations in this series published in Monticello, Illinois.

Bibliographic access by form of information product also presents some problems. Lists of periodicals, dissertations, and audio-visual materials are indispensable aids for the building and use of the gerontology collection. *The Survey of Periodicals in Social Gerontology and Geriatrics* (International Federation on Aging, 1976), would merit frequent updating. The *Journal of Gerontology* provides at times biennial and at times annual lists of relevant dissertations. Audio-visual materials and guides are occasionally reviewed in the *Gerontologist*. Topics on aging may be found in the audio-visual section of the *National Union Catalog* and the *National Library of*

*Medicine Audio-Visual Catalog.* The major monograph in this field is *Audio-Visual Aids: Uses and Resources in Gerontology,* edited by Ira S. Hirschfield and Theresa N. Lambert (Ethel Percy Andrus Gerontology Center, University of Southern California, 1978). It aims "to improve the quality of gerontological education through the effective use of audio-visual aids" and "to acquaint the professional with a wide variety of media, as well as to provide relevant information for quickly determining the appropriateness of a selection for a specific instructional purpose" (p.i). The book combines theoretical and practical approaches, and offers a review of pertinent research, selection criteria, assistance in constructing an evaluation questionnaire, guidelines for selection and use, and lists of producers and distributors. Media evaluations from Duke University's Key Word Index Collection of Training Resources in Aging (KWIC) project were also included.

While adquate retrospective bibliographic sources in social gerontology are available, access to the current literature is tenuous. The quarterly *Current Literature on Aging,* compiled and annotated by John Balkema at the National Council on the Aging Library is a welcome exception. One hopes this fine source will be expanded and better utilized in the future.

### Keys to Indexing and Abstracting Services and Databases

Users of special collections in social gerontology may use card catalogs, lists of periodicals and new acquisition lists as guidance to the holdings. The publication of the *Catalogs of the Ethel Percy Andrus Gerontology Center* (G.K. Hall, 1976), represents a well-known example. However, printed indexing and abstracting services and bibliographic databases are indispensable for accessing journal articles, conference papers, dissertations, legislative materials, research reports, and many other sources "hidden" in the holdings. The important role of printed services such as *Gerontological Abstracts* (University Information Services, Inc.) and, whenever available, their computerized counterparts, was emphasized by Emily H. Miller and Neal E. Cutler from the Ethel Percy Andrus Gerontology Center, University of Southern California, in their landmark paper, "Toward a Comprehensive Information System in Gerontology" *(The Gerontologist,* 16:3, 1976, pp. 198-206). One must consider that not all potential information users are fortunate enough to have a special collection in social gerontology nearby. In addition, not all users are gerontologists who usually have cross-disciplinary information needs. In general collections, gerontological information sources are scattered throughout the entire classification scheme of the holdings. In these cases, even a larger number of indexing and abstracting services and databases are needed to satisfy the aging-related information needs of users from a variety of disciplines and professions.

We will not attempt to compile a listing of relevant services because useful bibliographies of them already exist. Instead, we will focus on examples of these tertiary keys in order to assist the reader to find up-to-date information on relevant new indexing and abstracting services and databases whenever needed.

The first step leads us to bibliographies. In addition to the section on "Abstracts and Indexes" in the core lists by Edwards and Flynn, one can turn to *Library Resources in Gerontology: Periodicals, Indexes and Abstracts* by Patricia Pesaitis and Judith A. Hays (Wichita State University Gerontology Center, 1978). In the latter, guidance to coverage, arrangement, and relevant subject terms is offered. A very helpful section on selected indexing and abstracting journals and databases is included in Prisca Von Dorotka Bagnell's *Guide to Print and Non-print Media in the field of the Aging* (All-University Gerontology Center, Syracuse University, 1979). Notes on addresses, characteristics, publications, and user services offered by information systems are provided.

Keys to secondary indexing services include several effective directories of bibliographic databases such as *Computer-readable Databases: A Directory and Data Sourcebook* edited by Martha E. Williams, et al. (Knowledge Industry Publications, Inc., 1979) and *The Library and Information Manager's Guide to Online Servces* under the editorship of Alice Harrison Bahr (Knowledge Industry Publications, Inc. 1980). Directories may be supplemented by the latest guides and manuals of databased distributors, for example, the *BRS System Reference Manual and Database Search Guides* (Bibliographic Retrieval Service), the *Guide to DIALOG Databases* (Lockheed Information systems), and *ORBIT Quick Reference Guide* (Systems Development Corporation).

Library and information professionals looking for the most recent announcements of new databases may consult current issues of specialized journals, for instance, *Data Base, Online,* or the *Online Review.* Those, however, who would prefer a compact source to organizations that publish indexing and abstracting service and produce databases, could turn to the *Encyclopedia of Information Systems and Services* edited by Anthony T. Kruzas (Gale Research, 4th edition, 1980), regularly updated by *New Information Systems and Services.* Finally, readers who would like to locate research studies and evaluations of information systems, may find the *Annual Review of Information Science and Technology* (Knowledge Industry Publications, Inc. for the American Society for Information Science) interesting. We hope that gerontological information systems will be included in this excellent source in the future.

## Toward Socio-economic Data Sources

Involvement in programs for the elderly is producing large quantities of data at Federal and state agencies. Reports based on primary data on the economic, social, health, and housing conditions of the elderly are proliferating in both published and unpublished form. Access to this growing body of information presents a serious problem. In addition, as the U.S. General Accounting Office stated in its report on the "Conditions of Older People: National Information System Needed" (1979), more systematically collected and evaluated primary data are needed for policy decisions at the Federal level. GAO warned that "in the absence of such information, assessing the impact of various laws on the lives of older people is difficult" (p. ii). The report recommended establishment of a comprehensive national data system including information on the unmet needs of older persons, changes in their conditions, effects of Federal help, cost of help, and costs and benefits of alternative services.

Until such a system is created, primary socio-economic data will have to be obtained across the country by a number of publicly-funded and private research projects as well as from data banks in the Federal government. Much of this valuable information would remain in scattered files of agencies and academic institutions, were it not for the excellent program of the National Archive of Computerized Data on Aging (NACDA). Jointly administered by the Institute of Gerontology and the Inter-University Consortium for Political and Social Research at the University of Michigan, NACDA collects from researchers aging-related data sets produced by surveys, and announces their availability for secondary analysis in a catalog and periodic bulletins. Training programs are held to facilitate the utilization of data for research and planning.

In libraries and special collections, the need for statistical information on the aging often arises. In the following examples, we will identify a few relevant works which might be of some assistance in this respect. All of them will need continuous updating by the publishing source. The *Inventory of Federal Statistical Programs Relating to Older Persons,* compiled in 1979 by a Federal interagency task force, contains information programs within the Federal government which provide data on the elderly population. Included in each listing are the title of the program, the purpose, frequency and method of collection, publications and the person or unit to contact for further information. *The Guide to Sources and Uses of Current Data on The Aging,* written by Rose V. Siegel and Doris N. Drug (1974) for the Administration on Aging, describes how to obtain information about the states through Federal, state and local sources and provides guidance in the use of secondary data.

The National Council of The Aging published the *Fact Book on Aging: A Profile of America's Older Population* in 1978. Data on 1975 conditions were collected from Federal sources. The purpose was to consolidate data in various areas such as housing, transportation, and employment. The reader finds summaries and narratives which interpret the primary data. The U.S. Bureau of Census publishes *Current Population Reports* on the aging in its "P" series. One report of particular interest is *Social and Economic Characteristics of the Older Population: 1978* (Series P-23, No. 85, 1979). Among the subjects examined are demographic aspects of age, sex, race composition, and mortality. *Guide to Census Data on the Elderly* is the result of a study undertaken by both the U.S. Bureau of the Census and the Administration on Aging in 1978. Rather than presenting the data themselves, this guide leads the researcher to the proper census table, report or tape where data for specific needs may be located. *Characteristics of the Black Elderly - 1980* (Administration on Aging, 1980), provides statistical data from the U.S. Bureau of the Census, the Bureau of Labor Statistics and the Department of Health and Human Sevices, as well as analysis of the data. The *Social Security Bulletin,* issued monthly and in annual supplements, is a good current source for data on benefits, Medicare, and Medicaid. However, evaluations or interpretations are not included.

The Interagency Statistical Committee on Long-Term Care for the Elderly was convened in 1979 in response to data needs in a growing special sector of service delivery. The committee's charge was to inventory and assess existing and planned sources and make recommendations for new data collection efforts. *Data Coverage of the Functionally Limited Elderly...* (1980), and the *Inventory of Data Sources on the Functionally Limited Elderly* (1980), represent the important results of the committee's work and are available from the National Technical Information Service (NTIS).

## *Information Clearinghouses*

Without doubt, the Federal government provides an increasing amount of information for the elderly and for gerontological service, advocacy, education, and research. Policy reviews, special studies, legislative compilations, statistical reports, research results, descriptive brochures, and reference materials are produced in a steady stream. Some of the most prolific sources include the House Select Committee on Aging, the Senate Special Committee on Aging, a number of subcommittees, the Administration on Aging, the National Institute on Aging, and several advisory offices. In addition, materials on education, health, housing, nutrition, and other specialized topics are being issued by a large number of other agencies. Publications to facilitate consumer information and self-help for the elderly are especially noteworthy. The White House conferences in 1961, 1971, and 1981, are rich sources of policy studies and reports.

Although many of these diversified Federal documents are indexed by familiar reference tools such as the *Monthly Catalog of United States Government Publications,* the *Congressional Information Service (CIS) Index and Abstracts,* the *American Statistical Index* or the *Index to Government Periodicals,* the coverage is by no means comprehensive. The publication lists, catalogs, and bibliographies of almost all Federal agencies dealing with the social, economic, and legal aspects of aging should be kept in mind, although a search through them is necessarily a slow and fragmented process. *Subject Bibliography No. 39* published and updated by the Superintendent of Documents Office, brings together at least the major documents in this field.

There are special collections and related user services at the Federal level which need to be highlighted. The role of information clearinghouse, as these extensive pools of specialized information are called, has been described by the *Catalog of Human Services Information Resource Organizations* (Applied Management Sciences, Inc., and Cuadra Associates, Inc., for Project SHARE, 1980) as "facilitating the flow of the results of research to researchers, managers, practitioners, and the lay public" (p. x). Clearinghouses which began their rapid development and proliferation in the 1960s, may include in their functions collection building, literature analysis, indexing and abstracting, dissemination services and the digesting and interpretation of information. The role of intermediaries or information counselors who (a) identify and locate resources, (b) facilitate the process of problem-solving on the part of users, and (c) assist in the implementation of new processes, has been identified as crucial. Information counseling has been investigated by Anthony Debons in "An Educational Program for the Information Counselor" (American Society for Information Science, *Proceedings of the 38th Annual Meeting,* v. 12, 1975, pp. 63-64), and in Marta L. Dosa's "Information Counseling" (Science Associates/International, Inc., *Information Reports and Bibliographies,* v. 7, no. 3, 1978). Matilda Butler and William Paisley in *Communication for Change in Education, Interim Report* (Stanford University, Department of Communication, 1974), identified the three roles of information intermediaries discussed above. We may assume that the time-saving and use-facilitating service of information intermediaries in gerontology will become more and more important as the pressure of economies increases.

The National Clearinghouse on Aging, maintained by the Administration on Aging, began, in 1978, the development of a national network for aging information, called SCAN. The Clearinghouse's Service Center for Aging Information scans journals, reports, legislative materials, and other documents for its bibliographic data base which is available to all workers in the field. SCAN conducts custom searches and referral services, and provides copies of documents in the database for a fee. Sets of microfiche were sent to selected depository libraries, and bibliographies are being published. The *Thesaurus* (2nd edition, 1977), is in the process of revision. Bibliographic reference service is also provided by the Social Gerontology Resource Center, which is included in the SCAN system. Information about model projects is also available through SCAN's Program Experience Exchange.

Project SHARE, the National Clearinghouse for Improving the Management of Human Services, is operated by Aspen Systems Corporation under contract from the Department of Health and Human Services. It produces key monographs, for example, *Microcomputer Applications In Human Service Agencies* (1980), and bibliographies such as *The Family* (1980), and *Productivity in Human Services: Measurement, Improvement, and Mangement* (1980). The quarterly *Journal of Human Services Abstracts* includes numerous references to publications on aging which could not be easily located through any other source. Services and publications of Project SHARE are available without charge. The newsletter *Sharing* facilitates awareness and contacts between various projects and programs.

In the above mentioned *Catalog of Human Services Information Resource Organizations* (Project SHARE, 1980), many other Federal information clearinghouses eminently relevant to gerontological interests are listed. In the health field alone, separate clearinghouses provide information on alcoholism, arthritis, cancer, diabetes, the handicapped, food and nutrition, health education, health policy, high blood pressure, deafness, mental health, rehabilitation, smoking, and other research areas and service concerns. In addition to this invaluable catalog, other guides may be consulted as one starts an information search, for example, the *Information Market Place* (Bowker, biennial) and *Washington Information Workbook* (Washington Researchers, 1979), the *Directory of National Information Sources on Hand-*

*icapping Conditions and Related Services* (Government Printing Office, 1980), and the General Accounting Office's *Congressional Sourcebook* series (latest edition 1980), which lists the projects and programs that report on their activities to the Congress.

Information dissemination has established itself as a vital function also at the regional, state, and local governmental levels. If it is hard to piece together Federally generated information on aging, at the other levels, access to sources has presented an even more frustrating problem, and increasing governmental awareness of the value of information dissemination is a most welcome phenomenon. Ten Federal regional offices provide liaison with state and local activities, and are listed, together with state offices for the aging in *Information Resources in Social Gerontology* (Syracuse University, All-University Gerontology Center, 1979). Although some state agencies on aging have been operating since the 1940s, it was not until the Older Americans Act Amendments of 1973 mandated the delineation of state planning and service areas that the increased activities of designated state offices on aging began. "State plans on aging" are now submitted to the Administration on Aging for each fiscal year including a description of objectives, advocacy efforts, proposed state legislation, community-based services, a resource allocation plan, method of distributing funds, and advisory committee recommendations. These plans, together with other state documents and dissemination services, are prime sources of information on senior centers, older persons' organizations, and programs.

Area agencies on aging at the local level were created by the same legislation that affected the state offices. Hard-to-come-by local demographic and socio-economic data on the elderly, special studies, and handy brochures of useful facts are produced by the agencies in abundance. Information about area agencies and their activities is usually published by state offices on aging. Most country and city governments also supply aids to information and referral services in the form of directories of service, in addition to special reports and case studies of aging programs. Thus, what is called the "national aging network" of Federal, regional, state and local offices, is a rich resource of information. However, access points and the easy availability of documents need considerable improvement.

Although the concept of the information clearinghouse evolved from the Federal government, in recent years, gerontological associations, academic gerontology centers, research institutions, and advocacy organizations also began to offer some clearinghouse-type information services. Although many of these have not been designed as traditional information systems, in their direct approach to dissemination and familiarity with their constituents' needs, they very effectively augment the services of gerontological libraries and formal information systems. As economic exigencies of formal information facilities are mounting, the informal channels of agencies, organizations, and institutions are gaining in significance. It has also been recognized that human resources and expertise need to be linked into information sharing networks.

The National Gerontology Resource Center operated by the American Association of Retired Persons (AARP) and the National Retired Teachers Association (NRTA), provides database searches, reference service and referral, and has sponsored workshops on online information retrieval. In the second category of organizational Study of Aging and Human Development at Duke University; the Gerontological Information Center of the Ethel Percy Andrus Gerontology Center at the University of Southern California; the Cooperative Information Center for Hospital Management Studies at the University of Michigan, and the Gerontological Information Program (GRIP) at Syracuse University. This heterogeneous group of academic information centers either established on-going services or designed and evaluated prototype systems.

In the third category of examples, we refer to private research centers that disseminate gerontological information and sometimes provide assistance in information use in the form of workshops, for example, the Benjamin Rose Institute (Cleveland, OH), the Davis Institute for the Care and Study of Aging (Denver, CO), the Foundation for Aging Research (New York, NY), and the New England Gerontology Center (Durham, NH). Private organizations established to study, protect, and represent the interests and rights of the elderly comprise the fourth category of sources. Many of them carry out action or field research, mainly need assessment studies, sponsor advocacy programs and actively disseminate supportive information. Some are developing clearinghouse activities. Examples that come to mind are the American Council on Consumer Interest, and the Gray Panthers, composed of local groups and publishing the *Network Newspaper*. The National Association of Spanish Speaking Elderly (Associaciòn Nacional Pro Personas Mayores) which is engaged in social research and technical assistance to local groups and publishes *Legislative Bulletin* and *Our Heritage*, and the National Center on the Black Aged which also promotes the training of Black experts in gerontology, focus on problems facing the elderly in minority groups.

In order to identify the numerous organizational information sources that go beyond these few examples, one needs directories that supply a comprehensive enough profile of organizations including their conference activity, reports, monographs, journals, and newsletters. New organizations may be discovered in the updating service of the Encyclopedia of Associations (Gale Research, 14th edition, 1980), entitled *New Associations and Projects*. Although the scope of our essay does not permit us to explore the international scene, we would like to highlight the *International Directory of Organizations Concerned with the Aging* (United Nations, 1977, document no. ST/ESA/63 and publication no. E77. iv.10), and the current awareness journal *International Bibliography, Information, Documentation* (UNIPUB).

## Keeping Up-to-Date

In a field in which changes are rapid and the literature widely scattered, it is useful to have a few sources in mind where one can turn for updating information. Often called "current awareness" services, these sources include state-of-the-art reviews, accounts of advances in gerontology, bulletins and newsletters, and they might include services tailored to special needs such as selective dissemination of information (SDI).

The *Annual Review of Gerontology and Geriatrics* (Springer, v.1, 1980) aims to be a comprehensive source of scholarly information in the field. The first volume was edited by Carl Eisdorfer. Subjects include biological and clinical practices, and social and community services. The emphasis is on the critical assessment of the work and the evaluation of current research.

The Federal government is a good source for periodic reports in the area of aging. The Senate Special Committee on Aging publishes annually *Developments in Aging*. This is a book-length report on relevant legislation of the previous year, issues confronting the older population, and results of the implementation of Federal, state and local programs. Included in *Developments in Aging* is the annual report of the Federal Council on the Aging. Another annual report is published by the Administration on Aging which is required to report to Congress on its activities. Because the Administration on Aging is the umbrella agency for service-oriented Federal programs for the aging, its report is a useful source, especially when read together with the commentaries of advocacy organizations which appear in their various newsletters.

Inventories of recent and current research form an important category of updating service for researchers, policy makers and service providers. The *Journal of Gerontology* was launched in 1946 by the Gerontological Society of America with the goal of reporting new research and identifying problems in need of analysis. Although not a systematic inventory, the journal, together with the *Gerontologist* which covers more of the social aspects of gerontology, occasionally includes review papers of specialized scientific topics. One of the most widely used sources of abstracts of mainly unpublished research papers is also issued by the Gerontological Society of America. We refer to the *Program* of the Society's annual scientific meeting, a tightly packed volume of research summaries.

Central to research production and dissemination especially in the biomedical field, is the National Institute on Aging created in 1974 by the Research on Aging Act. NIA's annual report and *Special Report on Aging* provide an overview of NIA-funded projects and significant findings. Research efforts focusing on the social aspects of gerontology are often funded and disseminated by the Administration on Aging.

An amazing number of newsletters and bulletins are published across the country each week or month by organizations, private enterprise, and academic gerontology centers. We have chosen just a few examples. *AGHE* is the newsletter of the Association for Gerontology in Higher Education located in Washington, D.C. It brings us comments on issues and trends, and reviews books in the field. The National Indian Council on Aging publishes *News* on a quarterly basis. It provides information on legislative developments and events in aging which are of concern to Indian and Alaskan Native elders. *Aging Services News* is the product of a private undertaking which monitors legislative news, proposed government regulations, court decisions, and state actions. It is published bimonthly in Bethesda, MD, by Care Reports, Inc. *Aging Research and Training News*, by the same commercial publisher, announces grant sources, guidelines, Federal data resources, and some funded projects.

*Ageing International*, the quarterly publication of the International Federation on Aging in Washington, D.C. is available in English, German, French, and Spanish. It reports on innovative programs for the elderly world-wide and analyzes such universal concerns as euthanasia and health care. Announcements of international conferences, book reviews, and special issues devoted to topical reviews facilitate awareness. *International Senior Citizens* should be mentioned as the official bulletin of the International Senior Citizens Association, Inc., an organization "concerned only with making a life worthwhile for older people."

Area agencies and state commissions also publish newsletters and bulletins of interest to their communities. Academic centers which fuse education, research and service orientation, are prime examples of the producers of current awareness bulletins.

An overview of "Information in Social Gerontology" by Stephanie Ardito and Marta L. Dosa is provided in one of the forthcoming supplements to the *Encyclopedia of Library and Information Science* (Marcel Dekker).

## A Prologue to the Future

Instead of a futile attempt to review the major primary works in social gerontology in a short essay, we concentrated on categories of information resources that can discover and open up paths leading to existing and forthcoming primary publications, audio-visual materials, and information clearinghouses. We had to restrict ourselves to a few examples of these "keys" and omit any others we value. In bringing the informal information channels of organizations into focus, we wanted to emphasize the need for constant alertness to new developments in this fast-changing field.

The most important factor in supplementing special collections and information systems in social gerontology by the informal clearinghouse and dissemination activities of agencies and organizations, is cooperation. Only through intensive linkages among gerontological librarians, educational resource specialists, and information managers can we hope to access and utilize proliferating information resources for the benefit of the elderly.

# CANADIAN INFORMATION RESOURCES AND SERVICES IN GERONTOLOGY AND GERIATRICS

Elaine Duwors
Joanne Gard Marshall
Gale Moore

Research on aging has been carried on in most Canadian universities, community colleges, medical centers and social service organizations for many years. Individuals, or groups, working independently have been scattered across the departmental structure of their institutions and among institutions, in some cases with little or no contact with others in the community who share common interests and concerns. Unlike the United States, Canada does not have any large gerontology centers or institutes with substantial collections, nor does there appear to be any possibility of a major center with large collection being developed in the near future. Instead, gerontologists must rely on the large academic libraries or small special collections to meet their needs.

This article is intended as a sampling of the types of library collections and services which support gerontology in Canada. The first section of the paper will describe a special collection in geriatrics, the J. W. Crane Memorial Library of the Canadian Geriatrics Research Society. The second section will discuss the resources of the University of Toronto Library System and a proposal to enrich and improve access to these resources. The final section will deal with a program supported by the Health Sciences Library at McMaster University in which a clinical librarian uses the general collection to provide an information service to interdisciplinary health care teams, patients and family members in chronic care settings. While this article will focus on the collections and services of these three institutions, an Appendix has been included for readers interested in the state-of-the-art

Elaine Duwors is a Librarian, J. W. Crane Memorial Library; Ms. Marshall is a Clinical Librarian, Health Sciences Library, McMaster University; and Ms. Moore is Librarian, University of Toronto Library and an Information Consultant in the Programme in Gerontology.

of Canadian gerontology and the bibliographic sources for Canadian literature
on geriatrics and gerontology.

## The J. W. Crane Memorial Library

In 1955 a group of Ontario doctors and business leaders headed by Mr.
Harold S. Shannon, a prominent businessman and Dr. W. W. Priddle, Consultant in Geriatrics for the Ontario Department of Public Welfare, formed
an organization whose stated purposes were "to foster and direct medical
research into the causes and cures of ailments associated with the process
of growing old, the medical term for which is geriatrics." The organization was named the Ontario Geriatrics Research Society. The formation of
the Society was envisaged as a practical step in the fight against the health
related problems of the aged. Concurrent with the establishment of the Ontario Geriatrics Research Society, the Ontario Minister of Public Welfare
appointed an Advisory Committee on Geriatric Studies in 1958, chaired by
the Department's consultant in Geriatrics, Dr. W. W. Priddle. The Committee's duties were to improve medical care in homes for the aged in Ontario, to foster a program of activation and reactivation in these homes, and
to encourage research in the problems associated with the care of the aged.
The first duties of the Committee were to assist in the establishment of a
Provincial Geriatric Study Centre in a large home for the aged in Toronto,
Lambert Lodge, in order to improve the health care of residents in homes
for the aged in Ontario and to use any information collected to improve
knowledge of the medical problems associated with aging. Consultants in
the various medical specialties were appointed to the Centre to conduct clinics
for residents in homes for the aged in Metropolitan Toronto and the surrounding area.

As the Geriatric Study Centre developed, the need for a geriatrics library
for the consultants became apparent. In 1962, a geriatrics library was
established under the administration of the Minister's Advisory Committee
on Geriatric Studies. The nucleus of the library was a bequest of volumes
from the collection of the late Dr. J. W. Crane, at one time Dean of Medicine
at the University of Western Ontario, who had considerable interest in the
field of geriatrics and in the establishment of the Geriatric Study Centre. For
this reason, the library was named the J. W. Crane Memorial Library. The
library has always held an interest for the Board of the Ontario Geriatrics
Research Society. A substantial donation of books was made to the library
in 1965 by the officers of the Society, and in 1970 the Society undertook
to raise funds to update the library's collection on an annual basis. Late in

1970, negotiations were undertaken to transfer ownership of the library to the Ontario Geriatrics Research Society. In accordance with the bill of sale in 1972, a Library Committee was organized consisting of representatives of the Ontario Geriatrics Research Society and of the Ontario Department of Social and Family Services (formerly the Ontario Department of Public Welfare), to exercise and discharge the powers and duties of the Society with respect to the management of the library. A research librarian was appointed in 1970. The Onatrio Geriatrics Research Society was succeeded by the Canadian Geriatrics Research Society in 1975 in order to promote wider national interest in geriatrics across Canada. Currently the Society supports clinical geriatrics research projects in medical centers in many of the provinces, and is a major contributor to the financing of geriatrics research in Canada. The library was transferred to new quarters in 1979, along with the offices of the Canadian Geriatrics Research Society, and is presently housed with the Metropolitan Toronto Geriatric Centre (formerly the Ontario Provincial Geriatric Study Centre) and Castleview-Wychwood Towers Home for the Aged (formerly Lambert Lodge).

The library serves a wide variety of users including physicians, nurses, rehabilitation specialists, health and social service administrators, recreation leaders, social workers, health and social planners, social scientists, the media, and citizens. Institutional users include hospitals, homes for the aged, nursing homes, home care programs, universities and colleges, government agencies, medical centers, senior citizen's centers, and voluntary organizations. Students from many disciplines also use the collection. Borrowing privileges are extended to staff of the Geriatric Centre, the Ontario Ministry of Community and Social Services' (formerly the Ontario Department of Social and Family Services) senior citizen's consultants, and to the staff of charitable and municipal homes for the aged in Metropolitan Toronto and surrounding area. Special borrowing privileges are arranged by the Library Committee for interested agencies and individuals, and restricted borrowing privileges are extended to other libraries and information resource centers in accordance with the American Library Association Interlibrary Loan Code. Material may be requested in person, by letter, or by telephone and may be obtained in person or through the mail service.

The major focus of the library's collection is on the physiological and pathological aspects of the aging process and on the health care of the aged. The collection also contains works on the social and psychological aspects of aging. Reference materials include bibliographies, directories, legislation, and statistics, with an emphasis on Canadian data and sources wherever possible. Canadian government publications from federal, provincial, and local governments relating to aging are also included. The library is primarily a current working collection, with the majority of materials dating from the 1960s to the present with 1500 book and pamphlet titles, 1000 reprints, 115 periodical titles, and 100 vertical files. A collection of audiocassettes is being developed. Material in the collection is completely classified according to the National Library of Medicine scheme. In addition, an inhouse subject index to the periodicals in the collection is produced to provide speedy access to the journal collection.

The library is open between 9:00 a.m. and 5:00 p.m. Monday through Friday. Reading and study areas are available and a variety of reference services are provided. For example, the reference librarian will compile a specialized bibliography on request including materials in the collection and relevant materials located in other area libraries. Reference questions generally fall into one of three major areas: the process of aging; the health problems of the elderly; or social policy and services for the aged. Historical and geographical comparisons of subjects are frequently requested. The library also acts as a resource by providing information on upcoming conferences or referrals to individuals or agencies in the field.

## *University of Toronto*

In 1976, in recognition of the demographic changes that indicated that Canada, like other industrialized countries, was rapidly becoming ''old,'' the President of the University of Toronto struck a Task Force on Gerontology to investigate the teaching and research activities at this university. The Task Force recommended the establishment of a Programme in Gerontology; a program that would be independent of any faculty and with the administrative flexibility required to coordinate and encourage research in the field. The Programme in Gerontology, the first in Canada, commenced officially July 1, 1979. The Programme, in addition to serving as a coordinating office for activities at the university, sponsors a monthly series of research seminars bringing together researchers from a number of disciplines, and publishes a newsletter, *Focus on aging*. The newsletter which began in February 1980 provides up to date information on the Programme and on the gerontology related activities in the community. The University of Toronto offers graduate and undergraduate courses in gerontology in several departments. This pattern appears to be typical of other Canadian institutions as evidenced by a survey conducted by Gloria Gutman in 1977[1]; a survey now

---

[1]Survey of educational programs in gerontology and geriatrics offered at Canadian universities. Compiled by Gloria M. Gutman. Vancouver: President's Committee on Gerontology, University of British Columbia, 1977.

being updated by the Professional Education and Curriculum Planning Committee of the Canadian Association on Gerontology. In addition, there are at Toronto specialized programs in the Department of Community Health, Faculty of Medicine and in the Faculty of Social Work. A graduate diploma in gerontology co-sponsored by the Programme and Woodsworth College (a college primarily responsible for part-time studies) has just received final approval by the provincial government. The School of Continuing Studies and the Faculty of Nursing both offer continuing education in this area.

Resources, both print and nonprint, to support these activities and courses are held by a number of libraries on the campus. The central library system consists of two major research libraries, the John Robarts Library which houses the research collection in the humanities and social sciences and the Science & Medicine Library which has a similar mandate for medicine and the sciences. In addition, there is an undergraduate collection and more than fifty departmental collections. The Federated Colleges of the university all have extensive libraries and there are a number of departmental libraries which are not centrally administered and whose complete holdings are not available through a union catalogue. Finally, there are a number of reading rooms and "closet collections," some of which have extensive holdings, both in terms of books and journal subscriptions, which are supported by local budgets and are neither bibliographically controlled nor accessible. As most of the collections described are also physically quite separate, retrieval of materials can be time consuming for gerontologists who require access to a wide variety of subject areas. In 1976 the Central Library closed its card catalogue providing access to the majority of these collections through COM catalogues and an online abbreviated file, the CIRC system. This has the advantage of providing access from multiple locations; an essential link in such a large and disparate system.

Collection development for the central system is the responsibility of the Book Selection Department. Dealer selection plans are in place for North America, Britain, Europe, and more generally throughout the world. The department monitors these plans to ensure that coverage is complete as possible in all areas of interest, two of which are gerontology and geriatrics. These plans work well at the level of trade and commercial publications and it can be assumed that the current output of research materials are collected comprehensively. The Central Library collections are classified according to the Library of Congress Classification scheme and research materials are housed in either the Robarts Library or the Science & Medicine Library dependent on call number. There is some duplication of material necessary, particularly in the reference collections. For example, the Shock[2] bibliography is in both

---

[2]Shock, Nathan W. A classified bibliography of gerontology and geriatrics. Stanford: Stanford University Press, 1951. 1 vol. + supplements.

locations as is the Schonfield.[3] The Ethel Percy Andrus Gerontology Center catalogs,[4] on the other hand, are located only in the Robarts Library. The rapid rate of increase in the cost of subscriptions and the number of new journal titles appearing annually in all fields is creating a problem for Toronto as elsewhere. Strict control is being exercised over the placement of new subscriptions and as a result the serials proportion of the total book budget remains under 50%. In gerontology and geriatrics Toronto has to date been able to keep pace with new and continuing subscriptions but one cannot be too optimistic about the ability to retain this comprehensive coverage in the future. The field of gerontology now is covered not only by primary research journals but has added rapid communications publications such as the *Journal of clinical and experimental gerontology*[5] and review publications such as the *Annual review of gerontology and geriatrics*.[6] The Central Library has an extensive documents collection including both governmental and non-governmental organizations. Toronto is a depository for Canadian federal documents and Ontario provincial documents. Documents from the other nine provinces are collected selectively as are British materials. There is an attempt to collect American documents more comprehensively, either in paper or microform. Toronto is also a deposit library for a number of international organizations, e.g., UN, UNESCO, European Communities and has global subscriptions to many others, e.g., ILO, OECD. The Robarts Library has a special section where documents relating to the social sciences and humanities are housed. These documents are arranged according to a classification scheme originally developed at Guelph University and called CODOC, Cooperative Documents. This scheme arranges material by corporate issuing body and provides access by corporate body, title, personal author, if applicable, and a KWOC index based on title. Document material that falls into medicine or science is fully classified and integrated into the stack collection. Both the CODOC and the LC entries are included in the COM catalogues and the CIRC system. In addition, Science & Medicine and the Robarts Library both maintain vertical files. Materials considered ephemeral or of short term interest are housed here and include newspaper clippings, pamphlets, interim reports, etc. While there is not a departmental collection for gerontology or geriatrics, several of the departmental col-

---

[3]Schonfield, David and R. Stewart. A bibliography of Canadian research in gerontology, 1949–1969. Calgary: University of Calgary, 1970.

[4]Ethel Percy Andrus Gerontology Center. Catalogs. Boston: G. K. Hall, 1976. 2 vols.

[5]Journal of clinical and experimental gerontology. Vol. 1– , 1979– . New York: Dekker.

[6]Annual review of gerontology and geriatrics. Vol. 1– , 1980– . New York: Springer.

lections contain materials of interest. The Newman Industrial Relations Library, for example, maintains a special collection of books, pamphlets, bibliographies, legislative and statistical material and reports in the areas of retirement, pensions and the older worker.

The resources of the University of Toronto are vast and rich, but access in a multidisciplinary area such as gerontology is difficult. Due to the broad mandate of the university library, collection development does not go as deeply into some areas as might be desirable. For instance, the "grey" or fugitive literature; interim reports, committee reports, consultant's reports, etc. are not collected except on an ad hoc basis. Much of this material is not confidential, but access to it and awareness of it depends on an involvement in the process of research in the field.

What is required at Toronto is an information center for gerontology that draws on the wealth of resources available not only in the university but also in the community at large, and is staffed by a librarian or information officer who is directly involved with the individual researchers and staff in this area so that (1) access to existing collections can be facilitated, (2) the grey literature collected more comprehensively, (3) directories of resources—human, institutional, etc. can be compiled and maintained, (4) inventories of data sets, research in progress files can be developed, and (5) communication and cooperative information exchange i.e., networking, can be improved. The Programme is currently receiving a large number of requests for information, both directional and technical in nature, which it must handle and the need for a more formal information facility is keenly felt. The information center, on which some development has already taken place, would thus serve as a switch node or coordinating center furthering the mandate given to the Programme in Gerontology. As a prerequisite to the formal development of a system for the Programme a user study in which the nature of the research process, the current information channels and the information seeking behavior of those working in this multi/interdisciplinary field has been proposed and is currently awaiting a decision from the social Sciences and Humanities Research Council. The information system will be developed to support and enhance the information behavior of its users. Duplication of resources is no longer realistic; maximizing access is a positive alternative.

## *McMaster University, Health Sciences Library, Clinical Librarian Service*

In recent years, McMaster University located in Hamilton, Ontario, has formally acknowledged an interest in gerontology. A President's Committee on Aging was established in 1977 to advise on the future development of gerontology. Then, in 1979, an Office on Aging was set up whose purpose was to coordinate research and work related to gerontology throughout the university and to promote an awareness of these efforts in the various disciplines. Several years ago, an informal body called the Hamilton-Wentworth Group on Aging had also brought together health professionals, researchers, community service workers, and interested citizens who were interested in gerontology to share their common interest and to provide an opportunity for continuing education in aging.

The President's Committee on Aging included a librarian who was appointed to coordinate the library system's support of gerontology through its collections and services. There are four different libraries located on the McMaster campus. The Mills Memorial Library contains humanities and social sciences materials, including a number of special collections. The Thode Library has materials in the sciences and engineering, including psychology. The Innis Room serves the Faculty of Business, while the Health Sciences Library serves the Schools of Medicine, Nursing and other postgraduate and postprofessional programs in the health sciences. Since gerontology is interdisciplinary in nature, all of the campus libraries contain important materials which support the work of researchers and practitioners in the field. Our discussion here, however, will center around a specialized service which has been developed in the Health Sciences Library to satisfy the information needs of health professionals, volunteers, patients, and family members in the chronic care wards of the Chedoke-McMaster Hospitals, McMaster Division. Such specialized services which rely on the collections of academic library systems for support are less costly than the development of separate gerontology collections and may well play an important part in the future development of library support of aging in Canada.

The Health Sciences Library is located in the Health Sciences Center which was officially opened in 1972. The functions of research, education, and patient care are combined in one building with facilities relating to these functions spread throughout a thirty-acre floor space. Library support for faculty, staff, and students is given through a collection of 79,000 book and periodical volumes and over 7,000 audiovisual programs. Hospitals in the region are served through a Health Library Network which is funded by the District Health Council and located in the library. The clinical Librarian Service was introduced in 1975 to the Chedoke-McMaster Hospitals, McMaster Division to more effectively meet information needs in patient care settings. By participating in daily clinical activities such as conferences and bedside rounds, the librarian is able to identify and respond to information needs of health professionals, patients, and family members. Health professionals are provided with copies of recent articles from the biomedical literature that relate to current patient management problems, while patients and family members are given access to pamphlets and other suitable materials related to their health care. This service was expanded and positively evaluated under a grant from the Ontario Ministry of Health in four acute care settings during 1978/1979.[7,8]

During 1980, it was decided that the clinical librarian would be a useful addition to the health care teams on two newly opened chronic care wards. The clinical librarian began by attending all of the patient care activities on these wards which include kardex rounds held every ten days, admissions conferences with family physicians held after a patient has been on the ward for ten days, review conferences for each patient after he or she has been on the ward for six months, and death reviews. Nursing in-service sessions are also held every second week and a family group meets on a regular basis with the social worker once a month. Volunteers play an important part on the ward by developing special one-to-one relationships with patients. These volunteers get together monthly with the recreation therapist to discuss problems and share experiences.

There are a number of chronic care setting characteristics which contrast with the characteristics of acute care settings previously served by the clinical librarians. The patient population in chronic care is relatively stable and there is ongoing involvement of family members in the care of their relative whenever possible. Most patients and their families must deal with the effects of multiple continuing health-related problems rather than brief acute episodes of disease. These chronic health problems are often difficult for both patient and family to accept, especially if they involve physical and emotional behavior changes in the individual. Since many of the ongoing problems are not suited to active medical treatment, the nursing care provided by nurses and nursing assistants is of primary importance. The nursing staff comes to know the patients and their families very closely, providing support in a number of different ways. The allied health professionals such as physical therapists, occupational therapists, nutritionists, and social workers also have significant roles to play in maintaining the quality of life for the patients and their families.

These chronic care setting characteristics have influenced the nature of

[7]Marshall, J. G. "Clinical Librarians Join Health Care Team to Provide Information Directly." *Canadian Library Journal,* XXXVI (Feb./Apr. 1979), 23–28.

[8]Marshall, J. G. and Neufeld, V. R. "A Randomized Trial of Librarian Educational Participation in Clinical Settings." *Journal of Medical Education* (in press).

the clinical librarian service that has evolved in response to user needs. Longer patient stays and greater family involvement have resulted in the early development of consumer information packages on health problems such as stroke and glaucoma. The clinical librarian is not under the same time pressure to deliver information before the patient is discharged, hence it is easier to select and evaluate materials with the help of the patients and their families. Many family members have questions related to the hereditary nature of chronic conditions and, as a result, a larger proportion of the consumer requests come from family members than was the case in the acute care settings. Since a number of the patients suffer from dementias or other chronic mental disorders which limit their ability to participate actively in their own care and treatment, many family members feel a special responsibility to understand their relative's condition. This situation has also led to a greater volume of use of the clinical librarian service by family members. Since the clinical librarians working in acute care settings found that it was often difficult for patients to effectively understand and use information because they were feeling poorly or under stress due to an impending medical treatment, it may well be that family members are among the most appropriate recipients of this type of consumer health information service. Once family members have the information, they can share it with their relative at the best time and use it to better understand and cope with their relative's health problems themselves. Involving family members in the selection and evaluation of the educational materials is also a way of sharing skills that these family members have developed in helping their chronically disabled relative with other families who will need these skills in the future. The results of a survey of consumers using the Health Sciences Library have confirmed the observation of the clinical librarians that it is often the family member or friend who is actively searching for medical information rather than the patient.

The different nature of the health care provided in the chronic care setting has also affected the use of the clinical librarian service by health professionals. Nurses have become the predominant users of the service, followed closely by allied health professionals. Volunteers also use the service which was not the case in acute care settings. All of these health professionals, including the physicians, have shown an active interest in learning more about the process and problems of aging. A monthly printout of citations from the MEDLARS database has been started by the clinical librarian and numerous requests for articles on topics such as thyroid disease in the elderly, depression, and the effects of moving geriatric patients have been filled. These articles are placed in a binder called "hot topics" which is kept on the ward and a copy of the bibliography is placed on the staff bulletin board. In addition to the two or three articles on each topic which are made available in the binder, the clinical librarian lists additional print and audiovisual items available in the library. An important part of the service consists of library orientation sessions which are given to health professionals on the ward. These sessions are followed up with practical exercises in the library in which each health professional researches a topic for an in-service education session to be presented on the ward. Again, the fact that the type of health care problems being managed on the chronic care wards are long-term, has affected the clinical librarian service. There has been more time to develop a series of articles for health professionals on continuing problems such as the use of restraints on patients and the various diseases which affect older people such as Parkinsonism and dementias. Rather than responding to a critical need for a specific piece of information in a hurry, as was often the case in acute care, the clinical librarian has found herself giving more thought to the development of a systematic file of articles that will represent ongoing concerns regarding the care of the elderly.

Clinical librarianship is a relatively new concept whose origins barely go back a decade. Although this specialized service was first designed to assist health professionals in applying the latest information from the biomedical literature to acute patient care, it appears that there are other health settings in which the clinical librarian can operate. The flexibility afforded clinical librarians by their mandate to build a user-based information service can be used creatively to meet stated and perceived information needs in a variety of settings resulting in different, but nevertheless useful, products.

## REFERENCES

Aging in Canada: social perspectives. Edited by Victor W. Marshall. Don Mills: Fitzhenry and Whiteside, 1980. 314 p. Bibliography: p. 287–314.

Canadian Association on Gerontology. Newsletter. 1974– . Winnipeg: the Association. quarterly. Since 1976 has included the "Running Canadian bibliography."

Canadian gerontological collection I; selected papers 1977; Collection de gerontologie canadienne I; textes choisis 1977. Edited by Blossom T. Wigdor. Calgary; Canadian Association on Gerontology, 1977. 115, 96 p. Volumes 2 and 3 will be published in 1981.

Directory of long term care centres in Canada/Répertoire des centres de services de santé á long terme au Canada. Vol. 1– , 1980– . Ottawa: Canadian Hospital Association. Bienniel

Environics Research Group Ltd. The seventh age; a bibliography of Canadian sources in gerontology and geriatrics, 1964–1972. Ottawa: Central Mortgage and Housing Corporation, 1972. 290 p.

Focus on aging. Vol. 1– , 1980– . Toronto: Programme in Gerontology, University of Toronto. quarterly. A newsletter which includes a section "recent publications."

Rosenberg, Gilbert and Bernard Grad. Canada, *in* International handbook on aging: contemporary developments and research. Westport, Conn.: Greenwood Press, 1980, p. 39–59.

Schonfield, David and Robert Stewart. A bibliography of Canadian research in gerontology, 1949–69. Calgary: University of Calgary, 1970. 62 leaves.

# COLLECTING BOOKS ON OLD AGE

Joseph T. Freeman

A noted and dedicated bibliophile (are there other kinds?) once wrote that it was dangerous to put books on shelves because they are liable to breed. The warning must be true because acquisitions by book collectors seem to grow year by year almost faster than shelves can be found for them. In parallel, there is a growing number of collectors who take on this parenthood consciously with lack of awareness of what their new family responsibilities can involve.

Among some book collectors the trait is inborn or is stimulated by environmental forces. A few are exposed to teachers whose dedication to books acts as a pilot light even though ownership may be beyond the reach of some pedagogic salaries. Occasional collectors start as investors attracted by the promise of large profits and become trapped as library addicts. Some become involved in a way that is comparable to the story that if one wishes to bring down an enemy, the gift of a single orchid plant with a primer on how to raise them is effective. The dedication of a professional career to a special field of study may stimulate the collection of those books on which the annals and guidelines of the subject of a life's work rest. The zeal to add to a collection may become an urge that can range from pragmatic and scholarly interest to financial depletion. Finally there are those for whom the quiet quest for books and the solitude of a library recall what Prospero said, that "a library was dukedom large enough."

## The Fruits of Experience

These comments come to a point in books that deal with geriatrics and gerontology, as they would with any special topic. Geriatrics, a clinical science concerned with the medical care of the elderly, has had its major protagonist in the 20th century, Dr. I. L. Nascher (1863–1944) of New York,

Joseph T. Freeman, MD, of Philadelphia, is the author of *Aging: Its History and Literature* (NY: Human Sciences Press, 1979). This delightfully meandering and informal retrospective of the literature gives insights and clues that we have not wanted to clutter with bibliographical detail.—L.A.

who published his text under the heading of that term. In a brief biography of the author, it was stated that the term *geriatrics* first came to general knowledge with the publication of his book. It was true, but Nascher, at the time approaching the age of 80, apparently was keeping a careful eye on the literature. He commented in a letter that the date 1914 was incorrect because he had coined the word in 1909 and used it in a paper published in that year. His book was finished in 1912 but there were problems in getting a publisher to venture into a new field. Among his many activities, Nascher had founded the New York Geriatric Club in the same year that he finished his manuscript. He was working in a hostile environment and had major opposition to his ideas but lived to be named honorary president of the American Geriatrics Society. In his last year of life he gave a paper on *The Ageing Mind* at the Society's annual meeting. He was honored by his major pupil and close friend, Dr. Malford W. Thewlis, who was the founder of this Society. Since that time Nascher has received full credit for his foresight and talent. There is no dispute that he was deserving of the title of Father of Geriatrics, at least in the 20th century.

In his book of which the second edition was published in 1916, as well as in the 1919 text by Thewlis, a few pages are given over to the history of geriatrics in which are listed the names of men who had contributed to its development. Malford W. Thewlis (1889–1956) brought out the first edition of his book *Geriatrics* in 1919. It had six editions of which the last, *Care of the Aged (Geriatrics)*, was published in 1954. He asked Dr. Nascher to write the 1919 introduction. In addition to his many contributions to the field, Dr. Thewlis started a clinic and geriatrics hospital in Wakefield, Rhode Island in 1928 and was the permanent secretary of the American Geriatrics Society.

There was little of historical note on the subject until 1937 which is marked by a paper on the history of geriatrics followed closely by an important series of papers by Frederic D. Zeman, Burstein, Grmek, Gruman, Trevor Howell, Walter Doberauer, and D. Chebotarev among the many who were adding to this literature.

## *An Autobiographical Interpolation*

Personal involvement in the collection of works on all aspects of aging followed upon the decision in 1933 that geriatrics was deserving of special clinical study and possibly the choice of a career. At the time there were no guidelines. The Conference on Aging that was to be convened by Edmund Vincent Cowdry at Woods Hole was four years in the future. Emerging leaders were just beginning to find each other and to attract individuals such as Mueller-Deham who had been working fairly alone. For a young medical student then, there were no established rules, no trained advisers, no informed teachers, and no scientific organizations into which to fit. The result led to two lines of personal involvement, namely, clinical and historical. Tuberculosis in 1941 was a major epidemiologic problem and a study based on 3,000 cases was published under the title: *Geriatric Aspect of Pulmonary Tuberculosis*. The wrapper of the July 1941 paper had a typographical error that is not likely to occur again and undoubtedly was the result of the printer's unfamiliarity with the term; the word was spelled *geriatic* which was typical of the fact that in that period, every lecture on the subject and even the phonetics had to be preceded by a spelling on a blackboard, so that the typographical error was not unusual.

About the same time that the clinical study began, it was felt that a knowledge of the literature would require readings in the subject's history as the best self-schooling for future involvement. The result was the history paper that was published in 1937 to which reference has been made. The German historian, Johannes Steudel, in his works on the subject said that this paper was the first in his bibliography.

In a sense, the two publications followed the dictum of Osler that in order to go to sea, charts were necessary (the history paper), but to put to sea without clinical experiences would be like failing to sail at all (tuberculosis paper). In addition they were prophetic studies for the career that was to follow.

Among collectors books about aging, old age, and the aged in all of their varieties acquisition had begun pragmatically as the result of the need to have their reassuring presence by which to become informed about all phases of the subject. The idea of them as valuable or cherished possessions was of later vintage.

For a clinician, medical texts of practical application are a first priority, but for a neophyte engaging in the study of gerocomy, gerontology, and geriatrics, it was essential to locate useful directives at a time when there was minimal guidance in contrast to the modern medical scene of close supervision, organized thought, and informed teachers. At the time, books were almost the only teachers, and self-instruction was the only form available. Dr. Oliver H. Perry Pepper, Professor of Medicine at the Medical School of the University of Pennsylvania gave two lectures annually in the '40s on the subject of geriatrics. Other clinicians such as Kotsovsky, Nascher, Thewlis, Vischer, Stieglitz, and Mueller-Deham were single workers whose books became important to a generation of students of geriatrics just as their efforts placed them in the roster of the history of the subject.

Retrospectively these earlier works were identified, almost ingenuously, as a means of personal inquiry and discipline for the validity of what the field would become and of determining the virtues of dedication to its service. On both scores, the concepts came to maturity. The clinical aspects have become established as part of medicine's organization and the historical aspects are an accepted part of the field's humanistic development.

The beginning of the collection of the books was not entirely accidental or unplanned although an element of both was involved, but it was not until later that it was appreciated that what started as a form of gerontologic education had taken on other values. The way in which the collection came about may be of value as a guideline for students, incentives for historians, and of interest to book lovers and collectors.

The years when the history and the clinical paper were published were a low point of world economics. Funds were hoarded, if there were any to hoard. Most hospital interns were not paid. Family resources were limited. Many medical students were carried along by their schools even if tuition fees were unpaid. There was little extra money available for the purchase of books. Book collectors and booksellers of works on aging had minimal experience or knowledge on which to establish costs for the volumes of the new topic. Except for a journalistic review of geriatrics in *LIFE* in 1941, the subject seemed to lag although Cowdry's important *Problems of Ageing* (note spelling) had been published in 1939. Rare books could be purchased for one-tenth or one-twentieth of their later value and recent figures are low in terms of future prices. Luigi Cornaro's *La Vita Sobria*, 1558, was obtained for $75.00. Floyer's 1724 *Medicina Gerocomica* sold for $80.00. In a major bookstore on the Left Bank of Paris, four important volumes could have been bought for $20.00 each from the owner who did not know then of the new field nor had he become aware of the growing interest in these books. The 1940-1950 purchases located one by one in book catalogues became a starting point for a collection in geriatrics and gerontology to which booksellers quickly became alert. This period was the start of a search for historical books on aging by a growing number of students of an emerging subject to which it is not possible to return for price, access, or innocence.

In my own saga, the first purchase was the *Fruits of Experience* by Joseph Brasbridge which is an autobiographical tale of an older man that has little scientific importance. With the Cowdry book, the several publications of the Josiah Macy, Jr. Foundation symposia edited by Nathan W. Shock, and the appearance of the excellent series of history papers by Zeman, the lines of emergence of the special book collection became apparent. Three valuable items of the times, and still of clinical usefulness to students, were the Cowdry, the English translation of Mueller-Deham's *Die Inneren*

*Erkrankungen im Alter,* 1937, that was translated into English (with Dr. Milton Rabson) in 1942 as *The Internal Medicine of Old Age,* and E.J. Stieglitz's important text, *Geriatric Medicine,* in 1943. It has been stated, and should be repeated, that students of aging, particularly those entering the field now, would do well to have some knowledge of these three books that put forth clearly many of the features that future generations of students should know. Each volume has long-term values. Few books since that of Durand-Fardel in 1854, for example, can match the clinical experiences of Mueller-Deham in Vienna. Robert Monroe's collection of data at Harvard on 8000 subjects published in Boston in 1951 was the type of quantitative base necessary to establish priorities for the growing clinical field.

Early books on aging commonly refer to the Bible, a number of Hippocratic aphorisms,and Galen's *De Sanitate Tuenda* in addition to some citations in the Chinese *Nei Ching,* papyrus records, and notes of some of the great physicians of India. Although necessary elements to a full bibliography of aging, most of them are beyond the scope of most collectors but many of them are available in major libraries in translation.

With the Renaissance in which Friar Roger Bacon played an important part, his contributions to the subject of aging were summarized in his work *The Cure of Old Age, and Preservation of Youth* (translated from Latin by Richard Browne, 1683). The famous Catalan diplomat and physician, Arnaldus de Villanova wrote *De Conservatio Iuventutis et Retardatione Senectutis* (1297) which was translated into English from Latin by Sir Jonas Drummond in 1544. In 1912 Charles Dana published a facsimile of the original Latin translation with a foreword about its distinguished author. The Dana bookplate added to its personal value. Bacon and Villanova were moving out of medieval era into the opening of the Renaissance during which the Moorish-Arabic influence began to recede and the great universities, scholars, and other leaders in western Europe were taking the reins of the humanities and forming the expressions of nationalistic cultures.

## A Little about Books Per Se

Books rarely are as simple as a bundle of printed pages bound in covers and identified by formal symbols. In the art of book collection which "is an ancient pursuit" in many forms as witnessed by the classical example of the library of Alexandria (200 B.C.–47 B.C.), technical terms have been developed for the details of identification. Knowledge of such points is not necessary for those who love to collect and to own books as a philobiblion expression or even to have a warehouse for special volumes that are destined to become the comfortable collected contents in a student's corner of a classical library.

In the collection of books on aging, divided professionally into the categories of gerocomy for the sociologic, geriatric for the clinical, and gerontologic for the biologic divisions of the science, some volumes have taken on particular value. For example, there is the 1744 Philadelphia edition of M. Tullius Cicero's *Cato Major*, a *Discourse of Old-Age with Explanatory Notes*, printed and sold by Benjamin Franklin. Mr. James Logan did the translation for his own amusement in his sixtieth year and also "for the entertainment of a neighbour in his grand climateric aet 63; 9 x 7." Logan was a very learned gentleman who had been William Penn's private secretary, and although unschooled in any formal sense, was self-taught, knew five languages, amassed a major library, translated the Cicero for the benefit of his friends, left his books to the populace, and has a fountain in a Philadelphia square named after him on a site where public hangings once took place which is adorned by magnificent figures sculptured by Calder. His friend Franklin, a practical and rising Philadelphia publisher and community-minded citizen, added in typical editorial fashion: "I have, gentle reader, as thou seest, presented this piece of Cicero's in a large and fair character that those who begin to think on the subject of OLD AGE (which seldom happens until their sight is somewhat impair'd by its approach) may not, in reading, by the pain small letters give the eyes should the pleasure of the mind in the least allayed." Franklin was 38 years of age and was credited historically with the invention of bifocals. His portrait wearing his invention is well-known.

Christian Hoffman's book *Longevity* was printed in New York in 1798. It had been the subject of years of search not only to obtain a copy but to know more about the man. Who he was or what was his background resisted all efforts at identification and purchase. The only copy known to the author was in the library of a famous gerontologist who had been casual about his possession and possibly not very concerned about its ownership except in a general sense. Repeated gentle efforts to purchase this item were unsuccessful although a quarter of a century went into the effort from the time that it first was seen. Fortuitously, or perhaps it is better to say graciously, as this chapter was being prepared, the owner generously made it available for the collection.

At another time, the rare book *Vita Sana et Longa, The Preservation of Health and Prolongation of Life, Proposed and Proved etc.* written by Everard Maynwaringe (1625-1699) that was published in London in 1669 suddenly appeared for sale in a book catalogue. It was a rare offer. Despite a substantial price, a request for its purchase went off immediately only to elicit the most distressing response that is common to all collectors who fail to get an item: Regret; Sold, and a major opportunity was lost. Maynwaringe studied in Cambridge, England, visited America, and received a doctorate of medicine degree at Dublin. He set up practice in London September 1663 as a "doctor in physick and hermetick philosopher". His colleagues regarded his as an empiric for his belief in his own compounds and one who held firmly to the belief that tobacco was harmful as were violent purgatives and bloodletting. His peers did not concur; his name fell into oblivion, and he died in poverty, passed over by the people of his times, and recalled only by one of the 16 books that he wrote.

A more fortunate experience followed an announcement in a book catalogue of the availability of a first edition of Luigi Cornaro's delightful volume *La Vita Sobria*, Padua, 1558 (v.s.) in which the purchase was successful. Cornaro (1467-?1566), possibly the illegitimate scion of a prominent Venetian family, had fled to Padua where he had a successful career as an architect. He married well and enjoyed a family of numerous grandchildren from his only daughter. At the age of 40 his health was so poor that he saw no future for himself because of his dissipations. With admirable discipline he re-oriented his personal hygiene along lines of exercise, nutritional restrictions, a good frame of mind, enjoyment of music, and contentment in his family and work. At the age of 83, he wrote on essay in which he described his successful methods of attaining health and longevity. The fourth section of the volume was written when he was said to be nearing the century mark. The book, brief because Cornaro believed that it would be more likely to be read, went through more than one hundred editions. Richard Mead of English fame, once possessor of the Gold-headed cane, translated the four chapters as did Joseph Addison of *The Spectator*, who was an admirer and commentator of the life and works of the so-called Apostle of Senescence. Among others, W.F. Butler of Milwaukee did the same in 1903. There are a number of flaws on the escutcheon of the noted Venetian-Paduan other than his birth. There are substantial doubts whether he was as old as he claimed to be but his book like his legend has survived for centuries. Whether he lived as long as he said he did is not important; the example that he set in diet, exercise, and attitude can be translated readily into modern terms. A copy in its original cover with the type as clear on the fine white paper as the day on which it was printed is a book that would grace any library.

In 1724, John Floyer of Lichfield, England, published his *Medicina Gerocomica; or, the Galenic Art of preserving Old Men's Health, explain'd:*

*in twenty chapters*, etc. It was printed in London, and has been called "the first treatise on diseases of old age." The statement is too broad but it was the first major work of its type issued in England. Floyer (1649-1734),who was knighted, was a friend of his townsman, Samuel Johnson, who, he said, had been touched by Queen Anne for the King's Evil. Floyer was an original thinker. He counted the pulse by a watch that he invented; outlined a diet for scurvy; advised about the values of balneotherapy with particular reference to cold water (psychrolousia); and had written about asthma with which he was afflicted. Gunn in 1934 described Floyer in an issue of the *Medical Press and Circular* as being one of the British masters of medicine. A copy of that paper has been obtained. The only known picture of Floyer is a line drawing that was found accidentally in a book in Oxford's Bodleian Library.

By good fortune a fine copy of Floyer's book was obtained, but the story has an unhappy ending. In the 1940s a Geriatric Club had been organized at a Philadelphia medical school by which to introduce the subject informally to senior medical students. The meetings were held at 8 o'clock in the morning, eased by refreshments, and centered around guests known to have made local contributions to the field of aging in law, medicine, social service, rehabilitation, civic activity, and others. In order to increase what already was a growing spirit of interest among the students, a selection of a dozen books from the private collection was placed on exhibition in the school library. Each volume and author was described on a facing card. When the exhibition had been gathered together and returned home, the Floyer was missing and had remained so to this day more than thirty years after the event—and its loss is marked on the bookshelf as well as in memory.

Another story has to do with Francois Ranchin (1560-1641), Chancellor of the Medical School of Montpellier in the 17th century. A catalogue was received announcing a book auction. Among the works listed there was the name of Ranchin for his *Opuscula Medica* with a reference in fine type to a chapter on aging. A bid was submitted for which the book was obtained at a low figure. Published in 1627, it was in excellent condition. The chapter on old age was 137 pages in length in Latin. Arrangements were made to have some of it translated by a classical student of Latin who almost classically was in need of funds. Ultimately, enough material was located to permit the preparation of a biography of the notable Chancellor who died in 1641 of the plague against which he was leading the health authorities of his city. Ranchin's name was mentioned in the authoritative texts of Zeman and Grmek. The purchase of his work make it possible to establish his place in the history of gerontology with a fair degree of satisfaction and also to have his book become a nice part of a growing library.

There are other interesting books and papers on aging of limited supply and distribution that can be sought. Students in many European medical schools for generations have been required to submit a doctoral thesis of dissertation for the accreditation of their degree. The Medical Schools of Paris and Nancy, for example, have lengthy lists of such theses. The student articles are printed formally, usually paperbound, and dedicated with substantial flourish to an influential and favorite (not necessarily synonymous) professor or professors. The formula varies. The literary panache may represent the first tentative step to get a foot on the lowest rung of the medico-scholastic ladder on top of which the professor sits like Simeon Stylites near Antioch on his 60 foot pillar. The simile is not too far removed from the pattern of medical school hierarchy and professorial tenure. On occasion some of these undergraduate efforts of which a number dealt with aging were found in catalogues of booksellers and ultimately had interested purchasers.

As examples, in 1732 J. H. Dummelius at Basel wrote a medico-philosophical inaugural dissertation: *De AEtate Senecta et Fato Senum* dedicated to God, Country, Parents, learned Faculty, Friends, etc.

In 1741, Jacob Martin at Lyon dedicated his inaugural medical dissertation: *De Fato Senili* to his father and faculty advisers. Permission to submit the thesis was granted by the authority of the school's Rector.

In 1840,, A. N. Gendrin was one of 12 candidates for a position in the Department of Pathology at the Medical School of Paris. His thesis for the competition was *De L'influence des Age sur les Maladies* addressed to the Professors of the Faculty of Medicine and members of the Royal Academy of Medicine.

At the School of Medicine of the University of Paris in 1867, C.-S. Douaud dedicated his thesis for a medical doctorate: *De la Dégeneréscence Graisseuse des Muscles chez les Vieillards* to his Uncle, Family, Friends, and members of the faculty that included the thesis President.

In Bordeaux, C. Jarjavay dedicated his 1887 thesis (autographed copy) *Quelques Considérations sur le Rheumatisme Articulaire Chronique particulièrement chez les Vieillards* to his parents, friends, and masters of the Faculty of Medicine.

In the year 1877 a thesis for his medical doctorate was presented by T. Philippeau (autographed copy) entitled: *Étude sur la Pleurésie Primitive des Vieillards* dedicated to his master and the President of theses.

These neatly printed papers are representative of this special type of work that were earnest expressions by young students anxious and eager to enter upon careers in medicine. A few of the articles and some of the authors achieved distinction. Among the authoritative gowned figures to whom the works were addressed or dedicated there are many whose names are recorded in medical history as the result of their status and accomplishments.

## An Historical Sequence in Brief

A number of important books referring to age that appeared over the centuries will serve as a literary shelf for the subject's library. The usual citations of Aristotle, the Bible, Hippocrates, and the work of Galen can be taken for granted with a brief exposition. In 1808, for example, the distinguished scholar, Thomas Taylor, translated Aristotle's (384-322 B.C.) *Parva Naturalia* from the Greek of which one edition had been printed in Padua in 1473. It will be recalled as a datemark that Gutenberg's name was associated with the first use of movable type in Western Europe in 1454 and by 1476, William Caxton, the great English name in printing, was well under way with his work. Taylor's translation, *The Treatise on the Soul*, etc., covered the chapters on youth and old age, on the length and brevity of life, and on life and death, in a handsome large volume. The titles of the chapter, promised more than their reading value.

The Bible, ca. 750 B.C., contains many references to old age, the length of life, a list of long-lived patriarchs, and hygienic rules for the sustenance of life and social regulation. One of the most touching stories is the dignity with which Barzillai of Gilead courteously declined the invitation of the Judean King David to spend the rest of his life in Jerusalem. The old man refused humbly because he was getting along in years with little taste for pleasure and felt that he would be a burden on the court so that he elected to stay in his own community among his familiars. Old Thomas Parr (1483?-1635), the Shropshireman who came to London on an invitation to see the king, Charles 1, did not decline, or possible could not because of his noble sponsor who was the second Earl of Arundel. He died shortly after his arrival and came to autopsy by the famous William Harvey. John Taylor, the poet, wrote of Parr as *The Olde, Olde, very Olde, Man* (1635).

The works of Hippocrates, probably a compilation that included the observations by the best known who was the second of the Hippocratic line (c. 460-c.370 B.C.) can be searched for many details about aging. Francis Adams translated *The Genuine Works of Hippocrates* in 1849. It contains numerous aphorisms that apply directly to the aging. In 1804 Auchier in Paris had listed the sicknesses of old age according to Hippocrates.

Galen (130-200 A.D.) was famous for his *De Sanitate Tuenda* that was known to England's humanist physician Thomas Linacre (1460-1524) whose translation from Greek into Latin, was completed in 1517, and who also founded the Royal College of Physicians under Henry VIII. In the six books, particularly the second, fifth, and sixth, there are descriptions of old age. One of the most resourceful books on old age was that written by James Mackenzie (1680?-1761) in which practically every reference to aging to his time is to be found. *The History of Health and the Art of Preserving It* was published in Edinburgh in 1758 and translated into Italian in Venice in 1765. It would not be possible to be informed about books on aging to that time without an assessment of this volume that was printed by William Gordon. Parenthetically, the third edition contained a description of smallpox inoculation recalling that Benjamin Franklin's first legitimate son died of smallpox; Franklin regretted all of his life that he had failed to have the child inoculated. Mackenzie, whose book is divided into two parts, was a Fellow of the Royal College of Physicians of Edinburgh. The first section has an historical description of all aspects of food as they evolved from the primitive dietary of cereals and grains to more sophisticated meals of later culture. He cited many aspects of diet, exercise, and other rules as *gerocomice*, or the care of old age. In the second part, having referred to the work of the early Hebraic times, Greece, Egypt, and Arabia, up to his time in England with lists of names of the major figures who had contributed to the subject, he outlined rules of health. The book that was published three years before his death made appropriate mention of the School of Salerno, the physiology studies of Santorio, the temperance of Cornaro, and the points of view of many British authors. He commented that the book was "an account of all that has been recommended by physicians and philosophers towards the preservation of health from the most remote antiquity to this time. To which is subjoined a succinct view of the principle rules related to the subject, together with the reasons on which these rules are founded." This book by Mackenzie with the comprehensive summaries by Sinclair (1804), the bibliographies of Choulant (1791-1861), von Haller (1708-1777), and Canstatt (1807-1850) contain most of the views of old age and longevity with names and abstracts of the important contributors to the subject through the first half of the 19th century.

Prominent mention is made in these bibliographies of the popular medical work of Sir Thomas Elyot (?1490-1546) who was not a physician but a diplomat interested in political philosophy and the theory of education. The book was *The Castel of Helth gathered and made . . . out of the chiefe Authors of Physike, wherby every Manne may knowe the state of his owne Body, the preservation of Helth; and how to instructe welle his Physytion in Syckenes that he been not decyved*, printed in London by R. Berthelet in 1534 and said to have been dedicated to Oliver Cromwell.

Elyot's description of hygiene aroused the ire of the physicians of his day to which he replied that "before that I was XX yeres old, a worshipful phisition...read unto me the works of Galene...and afterwards by mine owne study I radde over..." many other authorities. His teacher may have been Thomas Linacre. Elyot was knighted in 1530. After the execution of Sir Thomas More, he retired to the life of a quiet student with the comment that he preferred this state to anything that a king could give him. In his book he outlined a regimen of living into old age in which he decried the use of excessive medications. He described a sensible approach to life with exercises, careful avoidance of infections, and sound psychological guidelines that may have been more important than what he learned from the study of the works of Hippocrates, Celsus, Pliny, Avicenna, Mesuë, and others who were the authorities on the subject of old age quoted in his time. Although self-trained in medicine from his readings he was equal to his similarly trained peers who had acquired the title of physician for a formal clinical career, but he was not recognized by them in any capacity.

Volumes could be written and long bibliographies prepared about all of the substances animal, vegetable, and mineral that have been used in an effort to promote longevity. The assumption, that is unwarranted, is that such accordion-expansions of the years of life will be accompanied by well-being, absence of diseases, fewer physiologic limitations, and perhaps above all, by the maintenance of erotic capacities. The literature tells of the use of human milk and many forms of soured animal milk, blood transfusions from young animals, immersion in various streams and fountains, orgasmal restraint, and the value of exposure to the beneficial health particles exhaled by young virgins. A reference to the last form will serve as an archetype of the many recommendations that have been made for the purposes of macrobiosis.

In the middle of the 18th century, J.H. Cohausen (1665-1750) served as physician to the Bishop of Munster in Germany's Westphalia. Stimulated by an inscription on a Roman tombstone that the interred had lived 115 years "by the breath of young maidens," Cohausen concluded that L. Clodius Hermippus had been a teacher constantly in the environment breathed by young girls whose exuberant health spilled over as distinctive particles into the air that they exhaled. He wrote a book, *Hermippus Redivivus: or, the Sage's Triumph over Old Age and the Grave. Wherein, a Method is laid down for Prolonging the Life and Vigour of Man.* The second edition that was translated by Dr. John Campbell into English was published in London in 1749. Of it Samuel Johnson cautiously advised that "if it were merely imaginary it would be nothing at all." Many others took the concept seriously; one physician rented lodgings in a boarding school after he read Cohausen's very convincing pages. This diversion of interest in books on aging, old age, and the aged can stand on its own values, and open a new area for collectors.

One of the great clinicians of the 19th century was Jean-Martin Charcot (1825–1893) whose major work on aging *Lécons sur les maladies des vieillards et les maladies chronique* was published in 1867 by Ball in Paris. The book consisted of a series of lectures on old age given at La Salpetrière in 1866 at which time he used the term *geromorphism* to describe the characteristics of the old body. The work was much more general than that of his noted predecessor, C.L.M. Durand-Fardel (1815-1899) whose *Traité Clinique et Pratique des Maladies des Vieillards*, published by Germer-Baillière in Paris in 1854, was a first-rate clinical presentation. The distinction and authority of Charcot gave his lesser work more prominence. The few lectures were of limited value until enhanced by Leigh Hunt's translation and the addition of a number of excellent chapters by Dr. A. L. Loomis published by W. Wood of New York in 1881 under the title *Clinical Lectures on the Diseases of Old Age*. Charcot made a number of important observations about aging and diseases including tremor, gout, rheumatic conditions, thermometry, and gave strong impetus to the science of geriatrics. This dramatic clinician, student of music, of Shakespeare, art, teaching, and research, throughout his career struggled against the belief that "ideas are more stubborn than facts." From the time of his popular lectures and the 1881 compilation, the field of aging moved forward along more defined clinical lines.

The fifth volume of Wood's *Medical and Surgical Monographs* was published near the end of the 19th century. The 1890 issue contained a paper on *Diseases of Old Age* by August Seidel. Aside from its merit as an important reference source that is available in major medical libraries, the forty pages treat the subject chronologically. A year earlier the same author had written on the pathogenesis, complications, and the treatment of the diseases of old age that was published in Berlin. More than a half-century was to pass before the views of Seidel and other German clinicians such as Mettenheimer (1824-1898) and Friedrich Friedmann of that period were equalled and then almost forgotten, to be surpassed only by the growth of technology available to the geriatric clinicians of the 20th century. Mettenheimer published his book in 1863: *Nosologische und anatomische Beitraege zu der Lehre von den Greisenkrankheiten*. Friedmann's work: *Die Altersveränderungen und ihre Behandlung* was published in Berlin in 1902.

In 1937, Ludwig Aschoff (1866-1942) published a series of papers in the journal *Medizinische Klinik* on the normal and abnormal anatomy of aging. His descriptions were comprehensive, objective, and of major value at a time when few such data were available. An English translation from the German was arranged privately but never published despite the importance of the material. Aschoff, a successor at the University of Freiburg to the famous pathologist, Ernst Ziegler, wrote an outstanding text on pathologic anatomy, attracted students from many countries, was noted for his pathology studies and views on historical subjects. His papers on aging were collected into a paperbound volume *Zur normalen und pathologischen Anatomie des Greisenalters* published in Berlin and Vienna in 1938. It is an important landmark between the clinical views of Nascher, the comprehensive compilation of Cowdry, and adjunctive to the excellent clinical text of Mueller-Deham.

As this narrative Odysseyan catalogue approaches the works of the 20th century, it must take into its account a number of more recent publications that have given shape to the development of aging's scientific organization. Nascher in all of the solitude of his early career has received proper recognition.

In 1890, Charles Sedgwick Minot (1852-1914) published his observations of certain aging phenomena that included studies by age of the weights of guinea pigs. In 1905 he gave the Harvey Lecture on the nature and cause of old age, and, two years later, a series of lectures at the Lowell Institute that were published in his volume, *The Problem of Age, Growth, and Death* in 1908. Minot was a foremost American anatomist and physiologist who had studied under the distinguished Karl Ludwig, Director of the Physiological Institute of Leipzig, who was called the Nestor of German physiologists by Osler for his contributions to research and teaching. With Minot's work the subject of aging obtained its modern introduction.

Alfred Scott Warthin (1866-1931), close to the end of his life, published *Old Age, the Major Involution; the Physiology and Pathology of the Aging Process* in 1929. He was professor of embryology and comparative anatomy at Harvard where he proposed a ''law of cytomorphosis'' for the progression of protoplasm into differentiated forms. He was quoted by Garrison as saying that science ''is at once the reality of human power, and the personification of human fallibility.'' His book in a special edition of 250 copies on Japanese vellum was dedicated to Dr. Francis Peyton Rous of which number 157 in personal possession has Warthin's handsome autograph. On its concluding page, Goethe was quoted to the effect that it is no art to getting old but it is an art to be productive.

In 1937 Albert Mueller-Deham (1881-1871) published his very important clinical work in Vienna to which reference has been made. A sound combination of ward rounds and compulsory attendance at autopsies on his old patients afforded this able clinician in internal medicine an opportunity for direct observations about the clinical and final aspects of old age. The author had come to the United States about the time that Korenchevsky, Henry Simms, Cowdry, Thewlis, and others were working toward similar objectives in the study of aging on national and international levels. The Gerontological Society and the American Geriatrics Society were chartered in the middle of this important decade of the 1940s. An international planning session in Liège, Belgium arranged for the first meeting of the International Association of Gerontology in St. Louis under the presidency of Dr. E. Vincent Cowdry in 1951.

Edward J. Stieglitz (1899-1956) was a clinician in Washington, D.C. and friend of Clive McCay from whose laboratory at Cornell major studies on aging primarily in the field of nutrition were being published. Stieglitz used his talent for leadership in Federal and independent organizational work on aging. His book: *Geriatric Medicine* was published in 1943 as the clinical counterpart to Cowdry's 1939 comprehensive volume. His firm editing and ability to obtain chapters from a number of competent clinicians was a forerunner of the multiple-author clinical texts that are in contrast to the single author-type of his predecessors. The book dominated the subject of geriatrics for years. No other American work of equal caliber was available for 20 years although there were many publications and new journals that served their respective roles.

## Terminus

After 1950, the number of books and magazines increased rapidly. In Shock's second supplement *Classified Bibliography of Geriatrics and Gerontology* for 1956-1961, 18,121 references were included. The search for items of value was made much easier by such competent listings in addition to the former cataloguing in the Index Medicus and individual bibliographies.

Coincidence, paradoxically, seems to be almost inevitable at least with regard to the availability and procurement of old books and theses. It is a dividend that often is unexpected to obtain a work in which there is the autograph of the author or a bookplate that is a herald of the provenance for known and unknown heirs. A book from the library of Dr. John Shaw Billings (1838-1913) who was founder of the Surgeon General's library (the first volume of its Index was issued in 1879) which became the National Library of Medicine, contained a rubber stamp of his signature of possession. The theses that often were autographed yielded insight into the customs of old ambitions now stilled, and printed pages that became lintels for the many established medical figures who were the recipients of the dedications. Just as the chance discovery of the Ranchin chapter led to the purchase of his book and the preparation of his biography, the guess that were letters of Nascher somewhere led to their discovery on which was based his biography that was published in the first issue of *The Gerontologist* edited by Dr. Oscar Kaplan in 1954.

These stories and those that every book lover can relate suggest that libraries at times must be the haunts of the Princes of Ceylon. As as example, as these notes were being reviewed and assembled in a noted medical library, a period of respite from labors led to the shelves common to all libraries on which there was a sale of a miscellany of old, duplicate, and outdated books for funds with which to purchase their successors. This casual effort turned up a copy of Dr. David Riesman's *High Blood Pressure and Longevity and other Essays*, Philadelphia, 1937, that was a 70th birthday anniversary celebration by his students and friends. It was a presentation copy signed by the author, obtained at a most reasonable cost and more treasured by the fact that the book's author had edited the first scientific paper of a young physician just entering practice, and the distinguished Professor of Medicine at the University of Pennsylvania had done so with teutonic firmness through six drafts finally down to a seventh that stressed punctuation in an approved text.

New library mechanics and technology are changing the world of books. The ironic 1751 observation is recalled that a library is the most striking conviction of the vanity of human hopes. Perhaps collectors of the future will purchase discarded, worn-out, and outmoded tapes of books as fitting collectibles. Unless all feeling for the past is dissipated, volumes in libraries, and their importance as guides to social accomplishments of culture, will continue to be history's safeguards just as all the efforts to preserve ancient monuments from the destructive effects of industrial pollution are continued. The floods of Florence that brought out an international response is a portent of the protective forces that appear constantly in the preservation of books, and book collectors are part of the protective phalanx. As a noted bibliophile wrote in 1936, ''after love, book collecting is the most exhilarating sport of all.''

In 1979, Arno Press recognized the importance to gerontology and geriatrics of the subjects' history. Under the direction of an editorial board, 36 volumes of distinguished books in the field were brought out in duplications of the originals and included *Roots of Modern Gerontology and*

*Geriatrics* selected and edited by Gerald J. Gruman in which a number of important historical papers were reproduced. As the subject of aging takes its place in a responsive society, the publications and people who created this awareness themselves have become a proper goal of collectors. A statement of 1775 will serve as an epilogue to this journey among the works on old age, namely, that "a man will turn over half a library to make one book" except, in this instance, it made one chapter.

## PARTIAL BIBLIOGRAPHY

Adams, F.: The Genuine Works of Hippocrates, London, Sydenham Society, 1849

Aristotle: See, T. Taylor

Aschoff, L.: Zur mormalen und pathologischen Anatomie des Greisenalters. Berlin u Wien Urban u Schwarzenberg, 1938

Bacon, F.: Historia Vitae et Mortis. London, J. Haviland imp. M. Lownes, 1623

Bacon, R.: The Cure of Old Age and Preservation of Youth (trans. from Latin F. Browne). London, T. Flesher, 1683

Brasbridge, J.: The Fruits of Experience - printed for the author, London 1824

Butler, W.F. (Publ.): Trans. of Cornaro's work (q.v.) with notes by Joseph Addison, etc. Milwaukee, Butler, 1912

Charcot, J.M.: Lécons cliniques sur les maladies des vieillards et les maladies chroniques. Paris, A. Deláhange, 1867

Charcot, J.M., Loomis, A.L.: Clinical Lectures on the Diseases of Old Age. New York, W. Wood, 1881

Cicero, M.T.: Cato Major, a Discourse of Old-Age with Explanatory Notes (trans. from Latin in English by James Logan and published by Benjamin Franklin) Philadelphia, 1744

Cohausen, J.H.: Hermippus Redivivus (trans. from Latin into English by J. Campbell) London Nourse, 1749

Cornaro, L.: La Vita Sobria. Padova, Perchacino, 1558

Cowdry, E.V.: Problems of Ageing. Baltimore, Williams and Wilkins, 1939

Douaud, C.S.: De la Degenerescence Graisseuse des Muscles chez les Vieillards. Paris, Frerer Dunan and Fresne, 1867

Dummelius, J.H.: De AEtate Senacta et Fato Senum. Basiliae Deckeri, 1732

Durand-Fardel, C.M.: Traite Clinique et Pratique des Maladies des Viellards. Paris, Germer-Baillière, 1854

Elyot, Sir T.: The Castel of Helth, etc. London T. Berthelet, 1534

Floyer, Sir J.: Medicina Gerocomica: or, the Galenic Art of Preserving Old Men's Health...London, J. Isted, 1724

Freeman, J.T.: Aging: Its History and Literature. New York, Human Sciences Press, 1979

Freeman, J.T.: The history of geriatrics. *Ann Med. Hist., 10:324-335, 1938*

Freeman, J.T.: The geriatric aspect of pulmonary tuberculosis. *Am. J. Med. Sc., 202*, 29-38, 1941

Friedman, F.: Die Altersveränderungen und ihre Behandlung. Urban u Schwarzenberg, Berlin u Wien, 1902

Galen: De Sanitate Tuenda (see, T. Linacre)

Gendrin, A.H.: De L'influence des Ages sur les Maladies. Paris, Germer-Baillière, 1840

Gruman, G.J.: Roots of Modern Gerontology and Geriatrics. New York, Arno Press, 1979

Gunn, J.: British Masters of Medicine, Sir John Floyer. London, Baillière Tindell and Cox, 1934

Hoffman, C.: Longevity. New York, J. Mott, 1978.

Jarjavay, C.: Quelques Considerations sur le Rheumatisme Articulaire Chroniuqe particulière-
ment chez les Vieillards, Bordeaux V. Cadoret, 1887
Kaplan, O.: *The Gerontologist.* Vol. 1, No. 1, 1954
Linacre, T.: Trans. of Galen's De Sanitate Tuenda from Greek to Latin. Paris, G. Rubeum, 1517
Mackenzie, J.: The History of Health and Art of Preserving it. Edinburgh, W. Gordon, 1758
Martin, J.: De Fato Senili. Lugduni Batavorum J. Luzac, 1741
Maynwaring, E.: Vita Sana et Longa, The Preservation of Health and Prolongation of Life,
London, J.D., 1669
Mettenheimer, C.: Nosologische und anatomische Beitraege zu der Lehre von den
Greisenkrankheiten. Leipzig, Teubner, 1863
Minot, C.S.: The Problem of Age, Growth, and Death. New York, G.P. Putnam's Sons, 1908
Monroe, R.T.: Diseases in Old Age. Cambridge, Mass, Harvard Univ. Press, 1951
Mueller-Deham, A.: Die inneren Erkrankungen im Alter. Wien, Springer, 1937
Mueller-Deham, A., Rabson, M.: The Internal Medicine of Old Age. Baltimore, Williams
and Wilkins, 1942
Nascher, I.L.: The Ageing Mind. *Med. Rec. 157:* 669-671, 1944 (his last paper).
Nei Ching Su Wen, or, The Yellow Emperor's Classic of Internal Medicine (trans. Iveith 1).
Baltimore, Williams and Wilkins, 1949
Philippeau, T.: Etude sur la Pleuresie Primitive des Vieillards. Paris A. Derenna, 1877
Ranchin, F.: Opuscula Medica. Lyon P. Ravaud, 1627
Riesman, D.: High Blood Pressure and Longevity. J.C. Winston, Philadelphia, 1937
Seidel, A.: Diseases of Old Age in *Wood's Medical and Surgical Monographs*, New York, 1890
Shock, N.W.: Classified Bibliography of Geriatrics and Gerontology 1956-1961. Stanford, Cal.,
Stanford Univ. Press, 1963
Steudel, J.: Zur Geschichte der Lehre von den Greisenkrankheiten. *Arch. f. Gesch. der Med.*
*35:* 1-27, 1942
Stieglitz, E.J.: Geriatric Medicine. Philadelphia, Saunders, 1943
Taylor, J.: Annals of Health and Long Life. London, E. Wilson, 1818
Taylor, T.: The Treatise of the Soul (trans. from Greek to English of Aristotle's Parva Naturalia).
London, Wilk, 1808
Thewlis, M.W.: Geriatrics. St. Louis, C.V. Mosby, 1919
Thewlis, M.W.: The Care of the Aged (Geriatrics). St. Louis, C.V. Mosby, 1946
de Villanova A.: De Conservatio Iuventutis et Retardatione Senectutis, 1297 (trans. from Latin
into English by Sir Jonas Drummond 1544) Facsimile by Charles L. Dana. Woodstock,
Vermont, 1912
Warthin, A.S.: Old Age, the Major Involution; the Physiology and Pathology of the Aging.
New York, P.B. Hoeber, 1929

# BOOKS OF INTEREST TO SPECIAL COLLECTIONS
## OF ALL KINDS*

Compiled by Lee Ash, General Editor

(*Bibliographical citations by author, keyword, or subject follow this
review article. The number of the citation in the list appears in the text.
Prices are listed when known.)

The most astonishing happening for this column in the past quarter was
the arrival one day, in the same mail, of the four most permanently important books to be noted herein: a *Guide to the Hoover Institution Archives,*
Kearney's *The Private Case,* Paher's *Nevada* bibliography, and a book that
will be used most of all these, the Hazens' *American Geological Literature,
1669 to 1850.*

### Guides to Collections and Resources

Among unusual books of the quarter stands first the long-awaited
catalogue of the *The Private Case* (31), compiled by Patrick J. Kearney,
an annotated and perfected bibliography of erotica in the British (Museum)
Library, which is amplified by a scholarly historical Introduction of over
fifty pages by G. Legman, one of the most noted and published authorities.
Important as the book is—for setting bibliographical data exactingly—it is
hardly the least bit titillating. Even Legman's essay represents a new con-
servatism (for him), but scholars and collectors will long be grateful to Mr
Kearney for his patience and his determination to do better than and to correct earlier bibliographers. Less fun, but far more useful of course, is the
*Guide to the Hoover Institution Archives* (106), which gives standard-type
excellent brief descriptions of 3569 archival series in that monumental in-

stitution. Special strengths are in North American (primarily U.S.), Eastern European and Russian (USSR), and Western European materials, with much less (about 13% of the total) representation from the rest of the world. Russian collections date from the 1880s, and American from about 1919, similarly from Western Europe. Politics, government, diplomats, economics, and social materials predominate. A fine name and subject index makes the volume invaluable for beginning researches into this great historical collection. Judaica is represented in this essay solely by Saul I. Aronov's extremely interesting historical and *Descriptive Catalogue of the Bension Collection of Sephardic Manuscripts and Texts* (48) at the University of Alberta Library's Special Collections Department. Well illustrated, and including various cultural and geographical components, from the 17th to the 19th centuries, the catalogue is fascinating (and instructive) reading, even for those of us who seem not to be concerned with the subject matter. In all, the excellence of the book's design can be suggestive for special collections librarians who need to produce catalogues descriptive of unusual materials. Also from Canada (from the same publisher), and also limited to a particular culture, is the *Supplement to a Lithuanian Bibliography* (61) which, for its use, is published from typescript, in double-columns with unjustified right-hand margins—a perfectly adequate presentation of over 4000 entries (adding to the 10,000 in the original 1975 bibliography), usefully classified, with author and title indexes, and a locator list of serials analyzed. The Table of Contents is fully analytical also and provides an immediate key to a great variety of subject approaches. More restricted in its area and time frame is the *Guide to Brooklyn Manuscripts in The Long Island Historical Society* (18), describing over 600 manuscript collections in the major repository for Brooklyn's (King's County's) history from earliest times. This is an exemplary guide to a geographically limited collection and the note "How To Use This Guide" and the detailed name and subject index, make the whole volume helpful. Not a specific collection, as such, but collected in most libraries, is the *New York Times*. Three or four decades ago it was relatively easy for librarians and students to find "things" in the *NYT Index* volumes, but as the news and the newspaper became more complex so did the index and indexing techniques. Now Grant W. Morse, a librarian, has helped to make it all easier through his *Guide to the Incomparable New York Times Index* (71), which not only explains the *Index* but gives valuable hints and suitable explanations of some otherwise puzzling idiosyncrasies that concern the selection of headings (often quite different from catalogue entries), their subdivisions, and cross-references. There is an interesting historical description of early volumes of the NYT indexes, from 1851, which should be studied by all users of noncurrent series.

Although it is not really a guide or index to collections, we do want to mention the revised 25th Anniversary Edition of a famous catalogue, *Heralds of Science* (92), highspots "represented by two hundred epochal books and pamphlets in the Dibner Library," now part of the Smithsonian Institution. Important to all collectors and libraries, this book, like *Printing and the Mind of Man*, is a picture of one aspect of the intellectual progress of mankind.

*Dictionaries, Encyclopedias, Atlases, and Other Reference Books, including histories and biographies of particular subjects*

No atlases were received this quarter ("There are no snakes in Iceland!*).

We did get a most unusually illustrated volume, however, in Fred Getting's extensive *Dictionary of Occult, Hermetic, and Alchemical Sigils* (98), a book that will be of tremendous help to many different kinds of readers and researchers interpreting symbols, signs, and glyphs. The thirty-page Introduction is extremely interesting and explains the character and uses of these unconscionably difficult, complex, and often complicated symbols. The textual annotations are clear, succinct, and refer to an extensive list of authorities in a Bibliography of about 300 items in twenty pages. (What fun it would be to try to assemble a collection of these mostly out-of-the-way books!) Several special appendixes will be helpful to students concerned with particular authors of alchemical and occult works, and the complex Index to Sigils is based on the number and character of strokes that make their designs. The book supersedes most others, and includes some 9000 sigils and their provenance under about 1500 headings (from Absorbent Earth [two 18th century citations] to Zuriel, "Angel of Libra" [two 16th and one 17th century reference]). Replete with excellent cross-references, this is the ideal book to help work out a lot of puzzlements for scholars, scholarly astrologers, and other scholarly occultists—to say nothing of giving inspiration to designers, and pleasure to crossword addicts and doodlers.

We have a real Dictionary-type book in C. W. E. Kirk-Greene's erudite *French False Friends* (27), those Faux Amis, Mots-Pièges, and Treacherous Twins that trap students, embarrass linguists, and destroy translations. For example, speaking of embarrassment, "Embarrassé. Sometimes means embarrassed but frequently just in an awkward position, or hampered, confused. 'Je voudrais vous aider. . .mais. . .je suis vraiment embarrassé: I would like to help you. . .but. . .I am really at a loss'." It makes one want to throw

---

*I hope that some of our readers, and now more, will recognize this model of editorial brevity and conciseness in this translation from the Danish by N. Horrebow, *The Natural History of Iceland* (London, 1757): [Head:] "Chapter LXXII, Concerning Snakes. [Text:] No snakes of any kind are to be met with throughout the whole island." End of chapter, p. 91.

out the French dictionary (it is so embarrassingly imperfect), but it will be better to use this exciting word book along with it. Lots of words (and even more ideas and cultural history) that might be interesting are found in Lewis A. Erenberg's story of New York nightlife and the transformation of American culture between 1890 and 1930, *Steppin' Out* (4), especially in the chapter notes; along with this I note Don B. Wilmeth's *The Language of American Popular Entertainment: a Glossary of Argot, Slang, and Terminology* (26), which is fun to leaf through and will be used a good deal by librarians. I wish, however, that Mr Wilmeth had been able to include citations to specific sources of his informaion (other than his appended brief "Select Bibliography") and had suggested the time period when these words and terms were used. It would have been helpful too if there was some indication whether the words were the argot, slang, terminology, or even something else he has collected. I have learned a lot from these definitions (such as "Give him the skull" and "Madball"), but I am not sufficiently entertained by the explanation of cooch dancing! More research and more cross-references would have helped make this nice book better.

Phonetic forms, including all known standard, local, and archaic variants, of "about 12,000 different names of English counties, towns, villages, farms, fields, rivers, lakes, mountains, islands, and even street-names of some major English cities (such as Bristol, Leeds, and London)" that are current, obsolescent, obsolete, or archaic—back for about a hundred years, so as to include glossaries of the English Dialect Society (EDS)—is what we have in compact, detailed, and greatly referenced book, *A Pronouncing Dictionary of English Place-Names* (79), by Klaus Forster. Here is an example of the practical use of erudition, for this small volume will lend authority in all kinds of discussions about the pronunciation of English places, many of which are unrecognizable from their spelling (or their hearing), which is all we heretofore have known about them. Well, those arguments are over now!

A Gale book that will have considerable use at the library Reference Desk is the first edition of a *Pseudonyms and Nicknames Dictionary* (84), listing "pen names, nicknames, epithets, stage names, cognomens, aliases, and sobriquets"—as well as pseudonyms—of 20th-century persons. The latter limitation, though helpful in many ways, restricts use of the book to searching earlier historic citations. Emphasis here is on more modern "authors, sport figures, entertainers, politicians, underworld figures, religious leaders, and other contemporary personalities." For the pseudonymous and other kinds of names listed, each refers to the real name. A special feature of the list is that also, under the 17,000 original real names, are listed some 22,000 assumed names (authors account for about 40%; with 55% divided between entertainers and athletes). Thus one can find the seventeen names that were used by Marion T. Slaughter (1883-1948), the American country-western performer. Entries also refer to coded sources of information that are listed with full citation in the book.

These three months brought us three "encyclopedias"—two, as it were, wet and one dried out but far from dry. Complementing one another, hygroscopically, are *The Ocean World Encyclopedia* (72), and *Encyclopedia of Ships and Seafaring* (97), both of which are well done and interestingly illustrated. Both are for the non-specialist, the former treating of different aspects of oceanography, such as physical, geological, chemical, and biological, with explanations also of oceanographic instrumentation, hurricanes, international organization, and individual famous oceanographers. This is as complete a volume as most of us need in nonscientific libraries and for home reference to supplement our major encyclopedias. Good cross-references help it all to hang together and the entries are relatively easy to find with the help of a reasonable index. The book on *Ships and Seafaring* is rather different being specialized chapters by noted authorities on prehistoric boats, oared boats, sailing ships and yachts, exploration. Further chapters are on powered ships and submarines, warships, and sea warfare, navigation, diving and salvage, the sea as a world resource (covered better in the other book, above), famous ships in history, "complete"(!) guide to ship and boat types, and a rather limited lot of brief biographies of "Great Men of the Sea." All the authors are British and the text reflects a very British bias. Uneven in coverage, both in depth and scope, I am unable to be enthusiastic about it. There is very little that my own unrelated reference books don't tell me just as well.

Drying out, hygrographically speaking, I turn to *The Encyclopedia of Ancient Civilizations* (7), edited by Arthur Cotterell, a much more important book than the previous two, containing signed articles by 38 modern authorities, all of considerable attainment in their speciality, most being professors or museum-types in history, anthropology, religion, or linguistics. The volume is divided into sections on Prehistory, Egypt, West Asia, India, Europe, China, and America, and within these there are separate chapters by the specialist authors on different geographical areas or subjects, among the latter being religions, the alphabet, the intellect, etc. Maps and excellent illustration, along with lists for "Further Reading", and a fairly good index, make this a great book to read—too heavy for a hammock but fine for the fireside, and for reference in any season. It certainly proves that, in spite of technology, we haven't really changed very much nor progressed.

In the arts I will note four books. First a puzzlingly uneven but beautiful one called *The Book of the Piano* (78), which has to do with the history and development of the instrument, numerous famous pianists—composers, and performers—and their technique or pianistic relationships with their instruments, piano makers, "eccentric pianos," a chronology, a glossary, bibliography, discography, and index. Really a pot-pourri, mostly of likely interest to piano students and, possibly, suitable for some reference work. It will appeal generally to music students but probably not to musicologists. There are a number of unfamiliar illustrations and portraits, many in handsome colorplates, which give the book style and most of its attractiveness.

My second and third books both refer to sculpture. Hacker Art Books (one of the most courageous reprinters, I think) brings back Christopher Gray's 1963 volume on the *Sculpture and Ceramics of Paul Gauguin* (35), for which art librarians, collectors, and dealers will be very grateful. The price of the book is not excessive for this beautiful display which so expands our understanding, appreciation, and admiration of the Gauguin who is more familiar as a painter. This was an artist wholly at home with, fully understanding of, and totally aware of the inter-relationship of the art forms he used. By using sculpture and ceramic arts Gauguin was able to adapt and perfect the presentation of his vivid symbolism, as this book shows in its readable text and excellent pictures. Quite different, and far less plastic, is the art presented in *Romanesque Sculpture* (93), a sturdy Phaidon Book from Cornell. Evenso, this work of tremendous erudition by Professor M. F. Hearn tells us, far more than any other, about "the revival of monumental stone sculpture in the 11th and 12th centuries," stressing previous history, then the origins demonstrated through capitals and relief slabs, selected Sanctuary sculpture, archtectural sculpture, and, finally, deep study and analysis of the Great Portals, the latter reflecting theophany, "theology made namifest," and "spiritual truth in physical beauty." Hearn's aesthetic interpretations and understanding reflect a deep spiritual sensitivity and an expert forcing of sometimes excessive iconographic theorizing. Nevertheless, there are few books that deal with these matters as effectively and with such authority. The centuries under study become vibrant through Hearn's easy writing style, informative notes, and full references.

A fourth art book is actually the catalogue of an unusual exhibition held in the Spring of 1981 at the Flint Institute of Arts, in Michigan. *European Tools* (104) pictures and explains a series of artifacts produced by and for workmen from the 17th to the 19th century. Some of the tools seem very odd today but all of them preserve a fine sense of craftsmanship, utility balance, and artistic design. The catalogue has an informative and appreciative introduction by the Museum's director, Richard J. Wattenmaker (himself a collector of ironwork and one of the nation's leading art historians) along with a brief essay by Jan Firch on "Tools As Art." Alaska provides us with two geographic guides on *The Aleutians* (3) and on *Wrangell-Saint Elias, International Mountain Wilderness* (2). Both are beautiful picture books with especially good descriptive tests to explain the areas, and both have the authoritative imprint of The Alaska Geographic Society. *The Aleutians* is most likely to receive a great deal of attention. It is the finest work there is on this long string of remote islands extending from North America toward Russia and which remains familiar to American servicemen from WWII to those based there at present. Wild and beautiful, the military, economic, and touristic future of The Aleutians can be foreseen. This authentically written and excitingly illustrated book is sure to inspire greater interest in the islands. Its authoritative character provides libraries with the best that has been written about them. Unfortunately, the fine folding colored map that accompanies the book (with its pictorial historical chart on the obverse) lies loose and unattached in the book. Surely, it will soon be separated and lost from most copies. Further, a superlative *Guide to the Birds of Alaska* (14) illustrates and describes every species found in the 49th state. Written by Robert H. Armstrong and the staff of *Alaska* magazine, the color photographs and descriptive text are accompanied by reproductions of paintings by the outstanding wildlife illustrator, John C. Pitcher. This brilliant volume is the epitome of sound bird identification manuals and the best one for Alaska.

Literary "companions" are a popular form of relatively easy scholarship. I do not mean to be condescending in remarking so. A great deal of reading, understanding, and analysis must go into their compilation by the specialists who make them. It is, however, "easy scholarship" on the part of the consumer that can be criticized and the consumption of these books by students is less than admirable—especially since so many students make no effort to read or write today. Nonetheless, publishers are receptive to these books because they have a good library market as reference books. This is particularly true of such a companion as Norman H. MacKenzie's *A Readers' Guide to Gerard Manley Hopkins* (39), a poet who is rather difficult for modern readers not versed in the classic Greek and Roman writers, in biblical allusions, Roman Catholic liturgical practices, and the Victorian ambience. But Hopkins' rich production ought not be lost to those eager to pursue his brilliance. I like "reading" (skimming) this worthy *Guide* because, unlike so many other authorities, MacKenzie is not pedantic, he is readable and clear, and nowhere did I find him doing any more than explaining instead of interpreting. Would that other guides recognized their mission with similar success. *An Edgar Allan Poe Companion* (79A), by J. R. Hammond, is not the same kind of book at all but it can be justified outside the scope of my criticism above. The author, an H. G. Wells authority and Poe enthusiast, has written a short and rather lively ''Life'' preceding a ''Dictionary'' which describes briefly the substance of individual tales. The rest of the book is substantively literary evaluation of the Short Stories, Romances, Essays and Criticism, and Poetry, but emphasizes the historical development of individual titles rather than analyzing their literary qualities. There follows an identifying list of characters and locations in Poe's fiction, and an ''Appendix: Film Versions,'' 1909–1978, with a Select Bibliography and Index.

The historiographic integration of contemporary scientific and philosophical forces and their development toward intellectual advancement is demonstrated with great success in the fascinating *Taddeo Alderotti and His Pupils* (63), the story of two generations of Italian medical learning. Professor Nancy Siraisi's brilliantly researched book has used primary sources in a variety of collections and benefitted by the review and advice of numerous specialists. The congenial style in which it is written interprets the Bolognese learning of the master physician Taddeo and the effects of the continuum of his Aristotelian philosophy on six of his students whose individual works survive to reflect the result of Taddeo's and of their own learned intellectual reflection, each proving to be quite different and yet the same. Professor Siraisi's engaging and clearly delineated concept of the importance of tradition, the philosophy of modernization, and contemporary medical knowledge in the development of medical practice, is remarkable and provocative in a most alluring way. Some traditionalists may dispute or question her but her evidence is substantive and persuasive. Scholars of the Late Middle Ages and Early Renaissance will welcome Appendix I (106 pp.), a ''Register of *Questiones*,'' containing a large majority of the *Questiones* (in Latin) ''examined by members of Taddeo's circle in their medical works.'' Though the list is known to be very incomplete, I do not know of a similarly full record having been published elsewhere, except perhaps in the Vatican Archive at St. Louis University, which I think has to do with philosophical (not medical) works. The Siraisi book contains other special features and a full bibliography and index. Typographically, and in its overall design, this is a good example of the attractive press work of the Princeton University Press.

Worry is intense in the American world of series of ''Papers of...'' because of the so-called Reagan budget. The established series fear faltering and new ones must be troubled whether they will get out of their cradle years. Thus, we cite, with trepidation on one hand and enthusiasm on the other, the prospected five volumes of *The Papers of William Penn* (76), which, following some of the other standard editions that are underway, promises a treasury of new materials about Penn, the Friends, and Pennsylvania history. Volume One, published in 1981, covers the early years of development from his birth in 1644 through maturity and to 1679, with the first Penn item being some verse of 1660. A wonderful series of books is anticipated by this first full volume, and all historians will hope for the successful continuation of the set. A more American personality is presented in Oceana Publications' ongoing series about the Presidents: *James E. Carter, 1924–* (83), edited by George J. Lankevich, supplies us with a very useful chronology, selected important documents, and a list of bibliographical aids.

If what is, to me, the most interesting historical book of the past year is an indication of the capacity of American scholarship, we have nothing to worry about in that area. Lee Clark Mitchell, a very young Princeton faculty member, has developed his dissertation into one of the best and most unusual approaches to the question of American Destiny in *Witnesses to a Vanishing America* (4A). He demonstrates that the problems of ethology and the western advance were recognized for what they were long before Theodore Roosevelt, John Muir, and others spoke out. Indeed, public interest, and a spreading awareness that western progress left a trail of destruction, was vocalized by Cooper, Catlin, Melville and many more—painters, writers, politicians, and the clergy. Self-destruction then as now, though not always as well understood, was a major problem for Americans who saw the passing of native Indian cultures and natural resources as a result of the rise of villages, towns, and cities. Sometimes the nation's people reacted effectively but, in balance (or out of balance), not much was preserved. Nor will it be in the future. The thrill of this book comes in its graceful recognition of those many persons who did effectively preserve the cultural heritage of the Indians, the past of our ancestors, and some of the natural beauty of our country, early enough in the 19th century, mostly because they knew what the result of indifference would be.

A book that is difficult to read, but a real challenge to historiographical exposition, is R. William Leckie, Jr's *The Passage of Dominion* (38), which for most of us will seem more interesting for its methodology and interpretive techniques, reasoning, and logical presentation that it is (to my thinking) for its conclusions. The argument continues—with the prospect of still other important books in the offing—to figure ''At what point could dominion be said to have passed from the Britions to the Anglo-Saxons.'' Well, what can one say to the nonspecialist? Perhaps, ''Here it is, folks. Read all about it!'' and, in the reading enjoy the history of kings and their sorting-out. Is Geoffrey's *Historia regum Britanniae* history or pseudohistory? It is still conjectural.

Mummies and mummification have always fascinated generations of readers. Here, after a long wait for it, is *An X-Ray Atlas of the Royal Mummies* (66), edited by James E. Harris and Edward F. Wente. Until 1965, and not since the classic 1912 volume, *The Royal Mummies*, by G. Elliot Smith, has there been an opportunity for scientists to examine the famous kings' and queens' mummies preserved in the Cairo Museum in detailed study. In 1965 and later, however, through cooperation of the University of Michigan, Alexandria University (Egypt), and the United States Public Health Service (National Institutes of Health), Michigan teams have used very special equipment to utilize optically oriented X-Ray beams for the study of the mummies' paleopathological, craniofacial, and dental conditions in various dynastic periods. These scientific techniques are examples of some of the newer approaches used in modern historiography, which makes the book worthy of note by special collections administrators as much as for its medical, anthropological, and historical uses. A feature of the book, besides the clarity of the text and its 143 photographs, are the 299 radiographs and computer tracings and 57 color slides, 211 of all of the latter on five microfiches in a Permalife envelope in the back of the book. Truly a transitional volume in the passage from what the mummies read to whatever books may be like someday.

## *Bibliographies & Specialist Booksellers' Catalogues*

*Nevada: an Annotated Bibliography* (70) by Stanley W. Paher, is the most complete list ever compiled concerning "books and pamphlets relating to the history and development of the Silver State". With 2544 entries, the bibliography lists and gives good descriptions of hundreds of books that are both important and overlooked, revealing many new aspects of Western history, journals of people bound for California, miners, farmers, writings about Indians, etc. Several previous but incomplete lists on the same subject have now been superseded, and from 1845 to (a few) 1980 entries this is the most complete and carefully done work of its kind, with fully explanatory annotations. Periodicals (including serials) and a few other types of publications, as well as manuscripts, are excluded. There are a few other limitations, and the list is critically evaluative—"only the most important"— which leaves a few special fields which have or deserve separate bibliographies. There is a list of "Theses & Oral Histories," and a short "Addendum," along with a good Index.

A wholly different bibliography, unannotated, seemingly exhaustive, but intelligently classified, is *Sun Power* (101), an almost complete record of the technology of solar and wind power, but limited (if it can be called that) to 3635 descriptive entries of United States government documents only— in all their formats, and indexes of personal names, agencies, titles, identification numbers, OCLC numbers, GPO stock numbers, and NTIS numbers. Many different kinds of technological libraries will find numerous uses for this accomplishment by Sandra McAninch, Head, Government Documents, University of Georgia Libraries.

The greatest treasure of the whole year, I believe, is the no less than magnificent key to early American geology by a young Carnegie Institution scientist and his professional librarian wife, Robert M. and Margaret H. Hazen's *American Geological Literature, 1669 to 1850* (36), already cited in the literature as "HH" or "Hazen" with reference to one of its accompanying 11,133 item numbers. Detailed, frequently annotated, and marvelous for its cross-references to reviews relative to the entries, this alphabetical list (by author) provides admission to a disparate older literature which, like taxonomic research in other fields of natural history, is still a useful resource for researchers. A full subject index has helped me in four months of using the book and never once have I found an error. This is a great American reference work and "Not in Hazen" will mark truly unusual pieces published to the middle of the 19th century. The introductory essay gives an overall review of the literature that is far more concise and better than can be found in any modern encyclopedia.

The rise and prominence of interest in photographica in recent years has produced a whole new, critical literature and an accompanying lot of bibliographical guides, keys, etc. One new piece is a thoroughly researched *Bibliography of Photographic Processes in Use Before 1880* (77), compiled by M. Susan Barger, documented as far back as 1839, describing materials, processing, and conservation. Expertly annotated, classified, and with author and keyword indexes, whole new approaches to the important older English language literature is now available from resources never so adequately searched. Notice of this very serious volume is followed here with that of *A Geo-Bibliography of Anomalies* (8), by George M. Eberhart. It would not seem that bibliography could ever be out of this world, but that is exactly what these 22,100 separate events, grouped under 10,500 geographic place names refer to (including "phenomena accepted by 20th-century science but which are incompletely understood"), such as the subtitle notes, being "primary access to observations of UFOs, ghosts, and [nearly all] other mysterious phenomena," all pulled together with indexes by subject, observers' names, ship names, and ethnic groups (Indians and Eskimos). The thirteen-page Glossary categorizes and these phenomena and can be used as an authority list for subject headings and indexes. Lots of fun for everyone in this book!

A distinctive catalogue of an exhibition of 18th century pamphlets, mostly about religion and politics, entitled *English Dissent* (29), is a sampling of the Howey Collection at the University of Missouri-Columbia. It is an example of how library materials can be selected to support a textual description of an historical event through an accompanying explanatory theme, full annotations of the pieces displayed, and attractive illustrations. Subject specialists and special collections librarians will benefit from study of this 116-page catalogue. Another historical bibliography, *The Old South* (101), compiled by Fletcher M. Green and J. Isaac Copeland, is unannotated but classified into a minute and specific arrangement, and includes the CSA and border states of Maryland, Kentucky, and Missouri, with some material on Delaware. Mr. Copeland is Director Emeritus of the Southern Historical Collection and Professor Emeritus of History at the University of North Carolina.

Two more music volumes this quarter: *Music and Bibliography* (68) is a book of fifteen essays on a great variety of specialist aspects of historical bibliography, compiled in honor of Alec Hyatt King, and reflecting his interest in "the history and documentation of the printing and publication of music; collections—particularly those now in the British Library—and collectors; the life and music of Mozart." This is a substantial volume, several of the studies being basic to their subject. The other book is in the new "Greenwood Encyclopedia of Black Music," *Bibliography of Black Music*: Vol. I, Reference Materials (15), compiled by Professor Dominique-René de Lerma, Director of Graduate Studies in Music, Morgan State University in Baltimore. The list is unannotated but includes all aspects of music and discographies relating to Black contributions, arranged by a careful classification. Unfortunately, there is no author index, though there is an index to the section on "Dissertations and Theses," with authors' names under institutions. Each section of the classification has separate numbering of citations, which complicates referral citation.

There are two descriptive author bibliographies to note, both in the Garland Reference Library of the Humanities (Vols. 221 and 224 are what we got), respectively, *Flannery O'Connor* (73), by David Farmer, and *Laura Riding* (89), by Joyce Wexler. The O'Connor volume is a fully descriptive bibliography of all her works and miscellaneous contributions, while the Riding book also contains lists of criticism with descriptive annotations. Both volumes include facsimile and other illustrations. Then, of course, there is Beatrice Rick's compilation of a bibliography of secondary references to the works of *William Faulkner* (32),—over 8000 items—in sections on Biography, Works (practically everything ever written or said by Faulkner), Criticism, and Bibliography, with a Topical Index and an Index of Critics. Jeanetta Boswell's *Herman Melville and the Critics* (64) covers her subject's critics from 1900 to 1978; and Robert Milewski does the same for *Jack Kerouac* (49) from 1944 to 1979. The Kerouac bibliography is heavily annotated. All three of the books—Faulkner, Melville, and Kerouac—are in the Scarecrow Author Bibliographies series.

The catholic and eclectic taste of *George Santayana* is made obvious by the publication of the *Catalogue of [his] Library* (90). Although most of the books contain his critical holograph annotations there is no indication of their character and the catalogue is really only a description of each item, not of the marginalia. Careful future study of the books will surely reveal some interesting ideas about the philosopher Santayana's work as reflected in his remarks.

Many libraries have had an opportunity to work with Gale Peterson in the past eight or nine years as he talked around the country for the Organization of American Historian's project that continues to try for a new Union List of Newspapers. In *A Bibliography of Iowa Newspapers, 1836-1976* (43), compiled by the Iowa Pilot Project, Alan Schroder and his staff at the Iowa State Historical Society have produced a fine and very valuable guide to the local newspaper resources of a medium-sized state. We can all hope that other projects—either underway or contemplated—will be able to progress and bring this great undertaking to fruition for the benefit of universal scholarship; however, like so many others, this project was dependent on an NEH grant of $10,000 and matching funds.

In the list appended to this essay, I have included citations to a number of interesting catalogues from booksellers. There is only space, however, to mention two of them: first, the earliest of a three-volume offering, The Rendell's fantastically elaborate collection on *The American Frontier from the Atlantic to the Pacific* (6), dealing with "Explorations & Settlement to the Mississippi River." Ranging from prices under $100, there are autograph letters, manuscripts, documents, books, pamphlets, maps, and prints, that are extremely valuable (and expensive), such as "the earliest known privately owned map of the New World in South America and [with the same item] the earliest documented Peruvian treasure map of the New World known to exist" [1577–84]; ($125,000). This is a set most historically-minded bookpersons will want to subscribe to. It is wonderful reading with its sometimes two or three page descriptive annotations, and a great find at $15 a volume, 1981–82.

The other catalogue is from Charles B. Wood, III, best known as a leading dealer in photographica. In *Catalogue 47: Architecture and Related Subjects* (11), he works in another speciality for which he was trained, offering 517 selected titles, 313 published before 1900 and most of those very desirable for any collection. The greatest strength of this offering is in pre-19th century works, many relating to rural cemeteries and to landscape gardening. A delightful and well-annotated reference guide as well as a catalogue. We can squeeze in here notice of the Gotham Book Mart's very unusual *Postcard Collector's Guide to Reference Works* (81), a sales list mostly with descriptive annotations to 152 numbered and priced books that can help dealers and collectors of this specialized format of pictorial Americana.

## *Books About Books–Rare Books, Collecting, Essays, Biographies, &c*

Felix Reichmann, Emeritus Professor at Cornell, I believe to be one of our great intellectuals and even as it was a pleasure to learn from him as a classmate in library school more than forty years ago, so it is to learn from his book on *The Sources of Western Literacy* (65), Middle Eastern civilizations. Stressing the fact that "culture is integration", he leads us through the development of language as a tool of communication to its perfection in the written word. He then reminds the reader of a wider transposition through the polygenesis of writing and prototypes of the book. Easy reading, this exciting story and its close identity with cultural structures makes it very appealing for anyone who wishes to reflect upon the human mind and the book in conjunction with progress and humankind. Above all, we learn to consider again our debt to the Middle East, through Mesopotamia, Pharaonic Egypt, the Byzantine Empire, and the rest of Arab civilization. Reichmann's notes, and his bibliography, make for an extra-special lagniappe of reading.

*Power, Politics, and Print* (58), by Barbara McCrimmon, is the first complete telling of the horror story of the planning, development, and publication of the British Museum Catalogue, 1881–1900. It is a story of massive frustration, heroic leadership, concentrated work, confused administration, and ultimate accomplishment. Surely 19th Century British bureaucracy and pettiness were even worse than our own!

One of the most delightful of librarians, Howard H. Peckham, Director Emeritus of the Clements Library, University of Michigan, has written a very congenial book, *Historical Americana* (6A) that every librarian and all student assistants in Americana collections should be required to read. It is a fine introduction to the books from which early American history is written. Better than any similar work, it tells why these books were important when they were written, and why they are of lasting interest. For any reader, it will give a sense of understanding and purpose that, along with exposure to the books themselves, will make the study of Americana a lively and attractive occupation. Also of importance to the collecting and preserving of Americana, is the still relatively new art of using oral sources in local historical research. The art and its techniques are clearly described in *From Memory to History* (75), by Barbara Allen and William Montell, published (with the certainty of quality) by the American Association for State and Local History. This is a good addition to the literature and emphasizes some of the special problems of local description along with internal and external tests for examining the validity of folkloric elements, even allowing for embellishment, biases and prejudices, etc.

Two unusual men, Frederic Raphael and Kenneth McLeish, have issued a select guide to best books cum best thought or ability or some-such, and turned out a delightfully opinionated and controversial *The List of Books* (16), ''The'' being, of course, the most controversial concept of *The* List. Acerbic or congratulatory, their annotations are never monotonous; their criteria are stimulating, and their selection somewhat wild. It's really an enjoyable pastime—checking what you've read and being pushed to read things you'd never have thought about. And the 25 books for a desert island holiday—well!

In a recent issue of BiN (*The Bibliography Newsletter*, IX, 3–5, March/May 1981), Terry Belanger asks for a halting in the random publication of books about book collecting. He did, however, single out the excellence of G. L. Brook's *Books and Book Collecting* (17), issued by Westview Press in this country. And Terry is absolutely right until someone can come up with something different in the field. We still haven't read all the previous titles in this class but Brook is good though, very informative, reminiscent, considerate, up-to-date with trends, and enjoyable. Another book that's very fine and might be missed by bookpersons is *Collecting and Care of Fine Art* (12), by Carl David, which actually can be read as though books were the subject. Chapters, among others, that are pertinent to books talk about what influences prices, long- and short-term investing, the auction, provenance, insurance, appraisals, security, etc. This one does belong with essential titles and is not altogether duplicative of others.

*Special Collection & Archival Administration*

Some time ago, in *Library Journal* (July 1981, p. 1394), I reviewed Richard K. Gardner's *Library Collections: Their Origin, Selection, and Development* (59), and only because it hasn't been mentioned in this publication is there any need to say more about this, an intelligent text on basic library functions. It is an extremely good, practical, and thorough manual, emphasizing that the selection of library materials is a dynamic function and that acquisitions should be measured carefully in terms of their usefulness. In another work thoughtful librarians and library board members can familiarize themselves with some of libraries' most cogent problems by reading *College Librarianship* (52), which treats—in separate papers—of administrative matters, archives collections, collection development, problems of catalogue automation, government documents, building planning, etc., etc. With regard to the last subject, William Hubbard's *Stack Management* (57), published by the ALA, is a truly practical guide to efficient and safe shelving and to maintaining library collections.

*Information Handling In Museums* (67), by Elizabeth Orna and Charles Pettit is oriented toward the British reader, but most of the material is easily adapted for North Americans to use it effectively. It covers theoretical and practical concepts of catalogues, classifications, and indexes, their interrelationships, determination of information needs, equipment, management, use, and a series of useful case studies.

Would it were as easy to adapt to AACR2. Well, another book of British origin can go a long way toward helping us benighted sufferers, *Using AACR2: a Diagrammatic Approach* (51). Try it, you may indeed, like it. At least it provides a "pictorial" explanation and it's fun to follow the arrows in the diagrams. *The Joy of Cataloging* (55) is restored, however, in a delightedly collected lot of the ever-embattled Sanford Berman's "essays, letters, reviews, and other explosions" and whosoever neglects it (or sighs over Berman's iconoclasms) is lost and may rightly be said to be a dull one. Here's to enjoy, to laugh (and despair), and—best of all—to learn. It is absolutely the best reading a professional cataloguer can find.

We are happy, of course, about another Haworth Press release, *Sex Magazines in the Library Collection* (94), a scholar study of sex in serials and periodicals, edited by Peter Gellatly. It solves few problems but throws light on some, and can be assigned as important reading, especially for public librarians. Never scandalous or pornographic, it can be bought and circulated without fear. How ridiculous to even think of that! Also somewhat more sexually oriented is *Lesbian/Gay History Researchers Network Newsletter* (50) which special collections people will want to know about for its up-to-date notices of acquisitions, archives, organizations, etc. By the way, *Sex Magazines* (above) has several lists of similar publications, along with their often elusive addresses.

While mentioning periodicals, I want to insert here notice of *The Book*

*Mart: a Monthly Journal for Book-Buyers, Sellers, & Collectors* (15A), because not only does it have a long article on the librarian "George Edwards: 'Father of all Ornithologists'," but there is an almost definitive piece by Robert Warren Pohle on the problems posed by Poe's *The Conchologist's First Book*, often thought to be a plagiarism. The article is "Edgar Allen Poe as a Naturalist," and I hope it gets into the Poe literature and bibliographical detection anthologies.

Finally, I close this installment with SPEC's Kit 69: *Preparing for Emergencies and Disasters* (28), which any librarian will be foolish to neglect. We know too little about the subject anyway, and this kit of directives, examples, bibliographies, and case studies is a good beginning for our reading about what we must be prepared to do—come fire, flood, or war.

## BOOKS RECEIVED

All books received are listed here. Titles marked with an asterisk (*) have been commented upon in the preceding bibliographical essay. Listing does not preclude further notice in subsequent issues.

   1.  (Africa). Maack, Mary Niles. *Libraries in Senegal*:Continuity and Change in an Emerging Nation. Maps & Plan. xiv, 280pp. Chicago: American Library Association, 1981. $20.00

   2.  (Alaska). *Wrangell-Saint Elias*, International Mountain Wilderness. (Alaska Geographic Society Quarterly, Vol. 8, No. 1). Profusely Illus., Some in Color, and With a Separate Fold. Map. 144pp. [distr: Norm Bolotin, 130 Second Ave, S., Edmonds, WA 98020], 1981. $9.95

\*  3.  *Aleutians, The*. (Alaska Geographic Society Quarterly, Vol. 7, No. 3). Numerous Illus., Some in Color, and With a Separate Fold. Map. 221pp. Anchorage, [distr: Norm Bolotin, 130 Second Ave, S., Edmonds, WA 98020], 1980. $14.95

\*  4.  (American Culture). Erenberg, Lewis A. *Steppin' Out*: New York Nightlife and the Transformation of American Culture, 1890–1930. (Contributions to American Studies, No. 50). Illus. xix, 291pp. Westport, CT: Greenwood Press, 1981. $23.95

\*  4A.  (American Destiny). Mitchell, Lee Clark. *Witnesses to a Vanishing America*. Illus. xvii, 320pp. Princeton University Press, 1981. $18.50

   5.  (American Foreign Relations). Davis, Allen F., ed. *For Better or Worse*: the American Influence in the World. Illus. xiv, 195pp. Westport, CT: Greenwood Press, 1981. $29.95

\*  6.  *American Frontier, The, From the Atlantic to the Pacific*. Vol. I, Explorations & Settlement to the Mississippi River: Autograph Letters, Manuscripts, Documents, Books, Pamphlets, Maps & Prints (416 items for sale). Illus., incl. Fold. Plates. 329pp. To be 3 vols. [II & III prospected]. Newton, Mass.: The Rendells, Inc., [154 Wells Ave, Zip 02159], 1981 [–82]. Each volume, $15.00

\*  6A.  *Americana, Historical*: Books From Which Our Early History Is Written, by Howard H. Peckham. (Michigan Faculty Series). 193pp. Ann Arbor: University of Michigan Press, 1980. $5.95

\*  7.  *Ancient Civilizations, The Encyclopedia of*. Ed. by Arthur Cotterell. Illus., incl. Maps. 367pp. N.Y.: Mayflower Books [575 Lexington Ave., Zip 10022], 1980. $29.95

\*  8.  *Anomalies, A Geo-Bibliography of*: Primary Access to Observations of UFOs, Ghosts, and Other Mysterious Phenomena. Comp. by George M. Eberhart. Map. xlii, 1114 double-column pp. Westport CT: Greenwood Press, 1980. $59.95

9.  *Anthropology for Archaeologists*: an Introduction, by Bryony Orme. Illus. 300pp. Ithaca: Cornell University Press, 1981. $34.50

10. (Archaelogy). Cordell, Linda S., ed. *Tijeras Canyon*: Analyses of the Past. (Maxwell Museum of Anthropology. Publication Series). Illus. xix, 200pp. Albuquerque: University of New Mexico Press, 1980. $19.95; Paper, $9.95

* 11. *Architecture and Related Subjects*: Catalogue 47 [1148 annotated items]. Illus. [137pp., double-columns]. South Woodstock, CT: Charles B. Wood III, Inc., N.d. Inquire.

* 12. (Art). David, Carl. *Collecting and Care of Fine Art*. Foreword by Richard J. Boyle. xi, 148pp. N.Y.: Crown Publishers, 1981. $10.00

13. *Baseball's Best*: the Hall of Fame Gallery, Updated 1980 Edition, by Martin Appel & Burt Goldblatt. Ports. & Other Illus. 439pp. N.Y.: McGraw-Hill, 1980.

* 14. *Birds of Alaska, A Guide to the*, by Robert H. Armstrong. Profusely Illus. in Color and incl. Paintings by John C. Pitcher. 309pp. Anchorage: [distr: Norm Bolofin, 130 Second Ave., S., Edmonds, WA 98020], 1980. $15.95

* 15. *Black Music, Bibliography of*: Vol. 1, Reference Materials, by Dominque-René de Lerma. (Greenwood Encyclopedia of Black Music). xix, 124 double-column pp. Westport, CT: Greenwood Press, 1981. $25.00

* 15A. *Book-Mart*: a Monthly Journal for Book-Buyers, Sellers, & Collectors. Lake Wales, Florida (P.O. Drawer 72, Zip 33853). Monthly, $7.50 a year

* 16. *Books, The List of*, by Frederic Raphael & Kenneth McLeish. 160pp. N.Y.: Harmony Books [One Park Ave., Zip 10016], 1981. $12.95

* 17. *Books and Book-Collecting*, by G. L. Brook. 175pp. London: Andre Deutsch [distr: Westview Press, 550 Central Ave., Boulder, Colo 80301], 1980. $25.00

17A. (Bookseller's Catalogue). E. K. Schreiber. *Catalogue 8: Rare & Interesting Books of the 15th & 16th Centuries*. [96 times]. Illus. 78pp. Bronx, N.Y. [3140 Netherland Ave., Zip 10463], 1981. Inquire

* 18. (Brooklyn, N.Y.). [Sink, Robert, comp.] A Guide to Brooklyn Manuscripts in The Long Island Historical Society. 134pp. Brooklyn, N.Y.: Brooklyn Educational and Cultural Alliance [57 Willoughby St, Zip 11201], 1980. $5.00

19. (California). Houston, John M. *Sails to Raise*: a Pocket Account of the Early Days of the San Pedro Bay Area (Before 1900). 2d Edn, August 1979. Illus. [72pp.] AND: ————. *The San Pedro City Dream*, Part I, "A City Is Born", With "Some Problems With Piety" and "The Amazing Account of Miss Nettie" and An Historical Calendar. Illus. [80pp.] San Pedro, Calif.: San Pedro Historical Publications [1435 West 17th St, Zip 90732], 1979;1980. $3.50; $4.80

20. *Children's Books, Notable*, 1971–1975. 36pp. Chicago: American Library Association, 1981. $3.00

21. *Chinese Fiction, Critical Essays On*, Ed., With an Introd. by Winston L. Y. Yang & Curtis P. Adkins. xvi, 236pp. Hong Kong: Chinese University Press [distr: Seattle: University of Washington Press], 1980. $14.95

22. *Chinese Government Serials, Bibliography of, 1880–1949*. Comp. by Julia Tung. [527 titles; with Chinese Title Index, and Publishers Index]. East Asian Collection, Hoover Institution. 136pp. Stanford: Hoover Institution Press, 1979. $5.00

* 23. *Collectibles*: the Nostalgia Collector's Bible, by Bert Randolph Sugar. Illus. xvi, 368pp. N.Y.: Quick Fox [33 West 60 St., Zip 10023], 1981. $12.95

24. *Deserts on the March*, by Paul B. Sears. 4th Edn. 264pp. Norman: University of Oklahoma Press, 1980. $12.50

25. *Dickens, Charles*: Books from the Library of the late Leslie C. Staples, Offered for Sale [698 items]. [64pp.] London: Fuller d'Arch Smith, Ltd [37B, New Cavendish St, W1M 8JR], 1981. Inquire

* 26.  (Dictionaries). Wilmeth, Don B. *The Language of American Popular Entertainment*: a Glossary of Argot, Slang, and Terminology. xxi, 305pp. Westport, CT: Greenwood Press, 1981. $29.95

* 27.  (Dictionaries, French). Kirk-Greene, C. W. E. *French False Friends*. 197pp. Boston: Routledge & Kegan Paul, 1981. $18.95

* 28.  *Emergencies & Disasters, Preparing For* [in Libraries, Museums, etc.] (Systems and Procedures Exchange Center, SPEC, Nov–Dec 1980 Kit 69). 107pp. Washington, D.C.: Office of Management Studies, Association of Research Libraries [1527 New Hampshire Ave., N.W., Zip 20036], 1980. $15.00, plus $2 handling

* 29.  *English Dissent*: Catalogue to an Exhibition of Eighteenth Century Pamphlets, 18 October to 18 November 1979, by Margaret H. Howell & Charles F. Mullet. . . . Facs. Illus. ix, 116pp. Columbia, Missouri: Ellis Library, University of Missouri-Columbia, 1979. Inquire.

  30.  (Erasmus). Boyle, Marjorie O'Rourke. *Christening Pagan Mysteries*: Erasmus In Pursuit of Wisdom. (Erasmus Studies, 5). xiii, 174pp. Toronto: University of Toronto Press, 1981. $15.00

* 31.  (Erotica). Kearney, Patrick J., comp. *The Private Case*: an Annotated Bibliography of the Private Case Erotica Collection in the British (Museum) Library. Introd. by G. Legman. Fold. Facs. 356pp. Limited to 1000 copies. London: Jay Landesman, Ltd [159 Wardour St, London W. 1], 1981.

* 32.  *Faulkner, William*: a Bibliography of Secondary Works, Comp. by Beatrice Ricks. (Scarecrow Author Bibliographies, No. 49). xxvii, 657pp. Metuchen, N.J.: Scarecrow Press, 1980. $32.50

  33.  *Film On the Left*: American Documentary Film From 1931 to 1942, by William Alexander. Illus. xviii, 355pp. Princeton: Princeton University Press, 1981. $27.50; Paper, $12.50

  34.  Flaubert, Gustave. *The Temptation of Saint Anthony*. Trans., With an Introd. and Notes by Kitty Mrosovsky. Illus. 293pp. Ithaca: Cornell University Press, 1981. $19.50

* 35.  *Gauguin, Paul, Sculpture and Ceramics of*, by Christopher Gray (1963). 19 Color Plates and 165 Other Illus. With Notes. 330pp. N.Y.: Hacker Art Books, 1980. $75.00

* 36.  *Geological Literature, American, 1669 to 1850*, by Robert M. Hazen & Margaret Hindle Hazen. [11133 entries]. 430pp. Stroudsburg, PA: Dowden, Hutchinson, & Ross [distr: Academic Press, New York, N.Y.], 1980. $40.50

  37.  *German-Americans, The, In Minnesota, A Heritage Deferred*: Ed., With an Introd. by Clarence A. Glasrud. ["Proceedings From Two Conferences Sponsored by Concordia College"]. Numerous Illus. 168 double-column pp. Morehead, Minn.: Concordia College, 1981. Inquire.

* 38.  (Historiography). Leckie, R. William, jr. *The Passage of Dominion*: Geoffrey of Monmouth and the Periodization of Insular History in the Twelfth Century. xii, 149pp. Toronto: University of Toronto Press, 1981. $20.00

* 39.  *Hopkins, Gerard Manley*: A Reader's Guide to, by Norman H. MacKenzie. 256pp. Ithaca: Cornell University Press, 1981. $17.50; Paper, $8.95

* 40.  (Horology). Shugart, Cooksey. *The Complete Guide to American Pocket Watches*, 1981: Pocket Watches From 1809–1950 Included–Catalogue, Evaluation Guide–Illustrated. Ed. by Walter Presswood. Over 500 Illus., incl. Color Plates. 254pp. Cleveland, TN: Overstreet Publications [780 Hunt Cliff Dr, N.W., Zip 37311], 1981. $8.95.

  41.  (Indians). Green, Michael D. *The Creeks*. xvi, 114pp.; (AND:) Frank W. Porter III. *Indians in Maryland and Delaware*. Map. xix, 107pp. [Each subtitled: A Critical Bibliography]. (Newberry Library Center for the History of the American Indian Bibliographical Series. Anthropology. Native American Studies). Bloomington: Indiana University Press [published for the Newberry Library], 1979. Each, $4.95

  42.  (Indians). Hobson, Geary, ed. *The Remembered Earth*: an Anthology of Contemporary

Native American Literature. Illus. xi, 417pp. Albuquerque: University of New Mexico Press, 1981. $14.95; Paper $9.95

* 43. *Iowa Newspapers, A Bibliography of, 1836-1976.* Comp. by The Iowa Pilot Project of the Organization of American Historians–Library of Congress United States Newspaper Project. [Alan M. Schroder, Project Director]. [xxvi], 371 double-column pp. Iowa City: Iowa State Historical Society [402 Iowa Ave, Zip 52240], 1979. $9.00

44. (Japan). Kiyohara, Michiko, comp. *A Checklist of Monographs and Periodicals On the Japanese Colonial Empire In the East Asian Collection, Hoover Institution.* . . . [1565 items; Author & Title Indexes]. xviii, 334pp. Stanford: Hoover Institution Press, 1981. $11.95

45. *Jefferson and His Time:* Vol. IV, The Sage of Monticello, by Dumas Malone. Illus. xxiii, 551pp. Boston: Little, Brown, 1981. $19.95

46. *Jefferson Scandals, The,* by Virginius Dabney. Illus. 155pp. N.Y.: Dodd, Mead, 1981. $8.95

47. (Jordan). Helms, Svend W. *Jawa, Lost City of the Black Desert.* Illus. xvii, 270pp. Ithaca: Cornell University Press, 1981. $37.50

* 48. (Judaica). Aranov, Saul I. *A Descriptive Catalogue of the Bension Collection of Sephardic Manuscripts and Texts* [at the University of Alberta]. Illus. xv, 213 double-column pp. Edmonton: University of Alberta Press, 1979. $15.00

* 49. *Kerouac, Jack*: an Annotated Bibliography of Secondary Sources, 1944-1979, by Robert J. Milewski. . . . (Scarecrow Author Bibliographies, No. 52). Frontis. Port. by Bill Van Nimwegen. x, 225pp. Metuchen, N.J.: Scarecrow Press, 1981. $12.50

* 50. *Lesbian/Gay History Researchers* Network Newsletter (March 1981, No. 4). Illus. 27pp. Washington, D.C.: Washington Area Women's Center History Project [1519 P St., N.W., Zip 20050]. $6.00 a year; trimonthly.

* 51. (Librarianship). Shaw, Malcolm, et al. *Using AACR2:* a Diagrammatic Approach. Illus. viii, 199pp. Phoenix: The Oryx Press, 1981. $19.45

* 52. (Librarianship). Stevens, Norman D., ed. *Essays From the New England Academic Librarian's Writing Seminar.* vi, 224pp. Metuchen, N.J.: Scarecrow Press, 1980. $12.50

* 53. *Librarianship, College,* by William Miller & D. Stephen Rockwood, eds. 284pp. Metuchen, N.J.: Scarecrow Press, 1981. $15.00

* 54. (Libraries). Bayley, Linda, et al. *Jail Library Service:* A Guide for Librarians and Jail Administrators. 114pp. Chicago: American Library Association, 1981. Inquire.

* 55. (Libraries). Berman, Sanford. *The Joy of Cataloging:* Essays, Letters, Reviews, and Other Explosions. xii, 250pp. Phoenix: Oryx Press, 1981. $22.50; Paper, $16.50

56. (Libraries). Drazan, Joseph Gerald. *The Unknown ERIC:* a Selection of [over 500 Educational Information Center] Documents for the General Library. 231pp. Metuchen, N.J.: Scarecrow Press, 1981. $12.50

* 57. (Libraries). Hubbard, William J. *Stack Management:* a Practical Guide to Shelving and Maintaining Library Collections. Diagrs. viii, 102pp. Chicago: American Library Association, 1981. $7.00

* 58. (Libraries). McCrimmon, Barbara. *Power, Politics, and Print:* the Publication of British Museum Catalogue, 1881-1900. 186pp. Hamden, CT: Shoe String Press, 1981. $17.50

* 59. *Library Collections:* Their Origin, Selection, and Development, by Richard K. Gardner. 354pp. N.Y.: McGraw-Hill, 1981. $15.95

60. (Linguistics). Goffman, Erving. *Forms of Talk.* 335pp. Philadelphia: University of Pennsylvania Press, 1981. $20.00; Paper, $7.95

* 61. *Lithuanian Bibliography, Supplement to a:* a Further Check-List of Books and Articles Held By the Major Libraries of Canada and the United States, by Adam and Filomena Kantautas. xxviii, 316 double-column pp. Edmonton: University of Alberta Press, 1979. $15.00

62. *Los Angeles:* an Illustrated History, by Bruce Henstell. Profusely Illus. With Over 400 Photographs, etc. 224pp. 4to. N.Y.: Alfred Knopf, 1980. $25.00

* 63.  (Medical History). Siraisi, Nancy G. *Taddeo Alderotti and His Pupils*: Two Genera-
       tions of Italian Medical Learning. xxiii, 461pp. Princeton: Princeton University Press,
       1981. $32.00
* 64.  *Melville, Herman, and the Critics*: a Checklist of Criticism, 1900–1978, by Jeanetta
       Boswell. (Scarecrow Author Bibliographies, No. 53). xi, 247pp. Metuchen,
       N.J.: Scarecrow Press, 1981. $13.50
* 65.  (Middle East). Reichmann, Felix. *The Sources of Western Literacy*. (Contributions
       in Librarianship and Information Science, No. 29). 275pp. Westport, CT: Greenwood
       Press, 1980. $25.00
* 66.  (Mummies). Harris, James E. & Edward F. Wente. *An X-Ray Atlas of the Royal Mum-
       mies*, Profusely Illus., incl. 5 Microfiches cards. 403pp. Chicago: University of
       Chicago Press, 1980. $60.00
* 67.  *Museums, Information Handling in*, by Elizabeth Orna & Charles Pettitt. Illus. with
       Charts & Tables. 190pp. Hamden, CT: Shoe String Press, 1981. $21.00
* 68.  *Music and Bibliography*: Essays In Honour of Alec Hyatt King. Ed. by Oliver
       Neighbour. Illus., incl. Facs. xi, 256pp. Hamden, CT: Shoe String Press, 1980. $38.50
  69.  *Navajo Rugs, Old*: Their Development From 1900 to 1940, by Marian E. Rodee. Il-
       lus., incl. Color Plates. 113pp. Albuquerque: University of New Mexico Press, 1981.
       $25.00; Paper, $15.95
* 70.  *Nevada*: an Annotated Bibliography [of] Books & Pamphlets Relating to the History
       & Development of the Silver State, by Stanley W. Paher. Maps & Facs. Illus. xxv,
       558pp. Las Vegas: Nevada Publications [P.O. Box 15444, Zip 89114], 1980. $95.00
* 71.  *New York Times Index, Guide to the Incomparable*, by Grant W. Morse. Illus. 72pp.
       N.Y.: Fleet Academic Editions, Inc. [160 Fifth Ave, Zip 10010], 1980. Inquire.
* 72.  *Ocean World Encyclopedia*, by Donald G. Groves & Lee M. Hunt. Illus. xv, 443
       double-column pp. N.Y.: McGraw-Hill, 1980. Inquire.
* 73.  *O'Connor, Flannery*: a Descriptive Bibliography. (Garland Reference Library in the
       Humanities, 221). Illus. xix, 132pp. N.Y.: Garland Publishing Co., 1981. $20.00
  74.  *Oppenheimer, J. Robert, Shatterer of Worlds*, by Peter Goodchild. Profusely Illus.,
       incl. Ports. 301pp. Boston: Houghton Mifflin, 1981. $15.00
* 75.  (Oral History). Allen, Barbara & William Lynwood Montell. *From Memory to
       History*: Using Oral Sources in Local Historical Research. xii, 172pp.
       Nashville: American Association for State and Local History [1400 Eighth Ave South,
       Zip 37203], 1981. $12.50; Paper $9.50
  76.  *Penn, William, The Papers of*, Vol. I, 1644–1679. Ed. by Mary Maples Dunn &
       Richard S. Dunn, et al. Port. & Maps. xv, 703pp. Philadelphia: University of Penn-
       sylvania Press, 1981. Inquire.
* 77.  *Photographic Processes, Bibliography of, In Use Before 1880*: Their Materials, Pro-
       cessing, and Conservation, comp. by M. Susan Barger. [x], 149 double-column pp.
       Rochester, N.Y.: Graphic Arts Research Center, Rochester Institute of Technology
       [One Lomb Memorial Drive, Zip 14623], 1980. $37.50
* 78.  *Piano, The Book of the*, Ed. buy Dominic Gill. (A Phaidon Book). Numerous Illus.,
       Many in Color. 288 double-column pp. Ithaca: Cornell University Press, 1981. $48.50
* 79.  (Place-Names). Forster, Klaus. *A Pronouncing Dictionary of English Place-Names*,
       Including Standard Local and Archaic Variants. xxxvi, 268 double-column pp.
       Boston: Routledge & Kegan Paul, 1981. $30.00
* 79A. (Poe). Hammond, J. R. *An Edgar Allan Poe Companion*: a Guide to the Short Stories,
       Romances, and Essays. Ports. & Other Illus. xii, 205pp. Totowa, N.J.: Barnes &
       Noble Books, 1981. $27.50
  80.  (Poetry). Rothstein, Eric. *Restoration and Eighteenth-Century Poetry, 1660-1780*. (The
       Routledge History of English Poetry, Vol. 3). xiv, 242pp. Boston: Routledge & Kegan
       Paul, 1981. $35.00
  81.  *Postcard Collector's Guide to Reference Works*. [A bookseller's catalogue serving
       as a bibliography of 152 items; annotated]. 14pp. N.Y.: Gotham Book Mart & Gallery
       [41 West 47 St., Zip 10036], 1981. Request.

82. *Pound, Ezra, Identity in Crisis*: a Fundamental Reassessment of the Poet and His Work, by Alan Durant. x, 206pp. Totowa, N.J.: Barnes & Noble Books [81 Adams Drive, Box 327, Zip 07511], 1981. $22.50

\* 83. (Presidents). Lankevich, George J., ed. James [Jimmy] E. Carter, 1924– : Chronology, Documents, Bibliographical Aids. vi, 153pp. Dobbs Ferry, N.Y.: Oceana Publications, 1981. $12.50

\* 84. *Pseudonyms and Nicknames Dictionary*. . . . Ed. by Jennifer Mossman. xvi, 627 triple-column pp. Detroit: Gale Research Co., 1980. $48.00

85. (Puppetry). Miller, George B., et al, comps. *Puppetry Library*: an Annotated Bibliography Based on the Batchelder-McPharlin Collection At the University of New Mexico. xxiv, 172pp. Westport, CT: Greenwood Press, 1981. $29.95

86. (Reading). *Let's Read Together*: Books for Family Enjoyment. xii, 111pp. Chicago: American Library Association, 1981. $5.00

87. *Reading for Children, Popular*: a Collection of the *Booklist* Columns, by Barbara Elleman. 60 double-column pp. Chicago: American Library Association, 1981. $4.00

\* 88. *Reference Works Through Five Centuries*: An Exhibition. . . To Celebrate the Fiftieth Anniversary of the School of Library Science at the University of North Carolina at Chapel Hill. [24pp.]. Chapel Hill: Rare Book Collection, Wilson Library, UNC, 1981. Inquire

\* 89. *Riding, Laura*: a Bibliography, by Joyce Piell Wexler. (Garland Reference Library of the Humanities, 224). Port. & Facs. xxi, 173pp. N.Y.: Garland Publishing Co., 1981. $32.00

\* 90. *Santayana, George, A Catalogue of the Library of*, in the University of Waterloo Library. Comp. by Susan Bellingham. Introd. by A. Kerr-Lawson. Illus. 67pp. Waterloo, Ont.: University Library, 1980. Inquire.

91. *Science & Medicine*, Catalogue 53 (400 items for sale). [Comp. by Diana H. Hook & Michael Horowitz]. Illus. 189pp. San Francisco: John Howell, Books, [434 Post St, Zip 94102], 1981. Inquire.

\* 92. (Science History). *Heralds of Science*, As Represented By Two-Hundred Epochal Books and Pamphlets in the Dibner Library, Smithsonian Institution. Preface & Notes by Bern Dibner. 25th Anniversary Edition. Illus. 96 double-column pp. Norwalk, CT: Burndy Library & Washington: Smithsonian Institution [distr: N.Y.: Neale Watson Academic Publications], 1980. $14.95; Paper, $8.95

\* 93. *Sculpture, Romanesque*: the Revival of Monumental Stone Sculpture in the Eleventh and Twelfth Centuries, by M. F. Hearn. 160 Photographic Illus. 240pp. Ithaca: Cornell University Press, 1981. $35.00

\* 94. *Sex Magazines in the Library Collection*: a Scholarly Study of Sex in Serials and Periodicals. Ed., With an Introd. by Peter Gellatly. (Monographic Supp. to *The Serials Librarian*, Vol. 4, 1979/80). 142pp. N.Y.: Haworth Press, 1981. $19.95

95. (Shakespeare). Smith, Marion. *Casque to Cushion*: a Study of Othello and Coriolanus. 176pp. N.p.: Canadian Federation for the Humanities [distr: P. D. Meany, Publishers, Box 534, Port Credit, Ontario L5G 4M2, Canada], 1979. $7.95

96. (Ships). Houston, John M. *Early Excursion Ships to Santa Catalina Island*: an Account of the First Passenger Service. . . Illus. 32pp. San Pedro, Calif.: San Pedro Historical Publications [1435 West 17th St, Zip 90732], 1978. $2.50

\* 97. *Ships and Seafaring, Encyclopedia of*, Ed. by Lt Cmdr Peter Kemp. Numerous Color Plates & Other Illus. 256 double-column pp. N.Y.: Crown Publishers, 1980. $15.95

\* 98. *Sigils, Dictionary of Occult, Hermetic, and Alchemical*, by Fred Gettings. Illus. With Over 9000 Sigils. 409pp. Boston: Routledge & Kegan Paul, 1981. $40.00

99. *Skelton*: the Critical Heritage, Ed. by Anthony S. G. Edwards. (The Critical Heritage Series). 224pp. Boston: Routledge & Kegan Paul, 1981. $27.50

\*100. (Solar Energy). McAninch, Sandra, comp. *Sun Power*: a Bibliography of United States Government Documents On Solar Energy. xx, 944pp. Westport, CT: Greenwood Press, 1981. $75.00

*101.    *South, The Old*: [a Bibilography]. Comp. by Fletcher M. Green & J. Isaac Copeland. (Goldentree Bibliographies in American History, Ed. by Arthur S. Link). xvii, 174pp. Arlington Heights, IL: AHM Publishing Corp. [3110 North Arlington Hts Rd, Zip 60004], 1980. $17.95; Paper, $12.95

102.    (Theatre). Patterson, Michael. *The Revolution in German Theatre, 1900–1933*. (Theatre Production Studies). Illus. 232pp. Boston: Routledge & Kegan Paul, 1981. $29.50

103.    *Theatre, Victorian Spectacular, 1850–1910*, by Michael R. Booth. (Theatre Production Studies). Illus. ix, 190pp. Boston: Routledge & Kegan Paul, 1981. $29.50

*104.    *Tools, European, From the 17th to the 19th Century*: Woodworking, Metalworking, and Related Trades, by Richard J. Wattenmaker, Jan Firch, & Alain Joyaux. [Catalogue of an exhibit, 26 April–7 June 1981]. Numerous Illus. 76pp. Flint, Michigan: Flint Institute of Arts [1120 East Kearsley St, Zip 48503], 1981. Inquire.

105.    (U.S. Economics & Politics). Garreau, Joel. *The Nine Nations of North America*. xvii, 427pp. Boston: Houghton Mifflin, 1981. $14.95

*106.    (War, Revolution, & Peace). Palm, Charles G. & Dale Reed. *Guide to the Hoover Institution Archives*. (Hoover Bibliographical Series, 59). 418 multicolumned pp. Stanford: Hoover Institution Press, Stanford University, 1980. $75.00

107.    (Women). McNall, Sally Allen. *Who Is In the House?* A Psychological Study of Two Centuries of Women's Fiction in America, 1795 to the Present. xii, 153pp. N.Y.: Elsevier [distr: Greenwood Press, Westport, CT], 1981. $17.95

108.    Wordsworth, William. *Benjamin the Waggoner*. Ed. by Paul F. Betz. (The Cornell Wordsworth; Center for Scholarly Editions series). Ms Facs. Plates. Ithaca: Cornell University Press, 1981. $39.50

109.    Yeats, William Butler. *The Secret Rose*: a Variorum Edition. Ed. by Phillip L. Marcus, et al. xxxiv, 271pp. Ithaca: Cornell University Press, 1981. $28.50